Language Death in Mesmes

A Sociolinguistic and
Historical-Comparative Examination of a
Disappearing Ethiopian-Semitic Language

SIL International and
The University of Texas at Arlington
Publications in Linguistics

Publication 145

Publications in Linguistics are published jointly by SIL International and the University of Texas at Arlington. The series is a venue for works covering a broad range of topics in linguistics, especially the analytical treatment of minority languages from all parts of the world. While most volumes are authored by members of SIL, suitable works by others will also form part of the series.

Series Editors

Donald A. Burquest   Mary Ruth Wise
University of Texas at Arlington SIL International

Volume Editor

George Huttar
Johanna Felton

Production Staff

Bonnie Brown, Managing Editor
Lois Gourley, Compositor
Barbara Alber, Graphic Artist

Language Death in Mesmes

A Sociolinguistic and Historical-Comparative Examination of a Disappearing Ethiopian-Semitic Language

Michael Bryan Ahland

SIL International
and
The University of Texas at Arlington

©2010 by SIL International
Library of Congress Catalog No: 2009935033
ISBN: 978-1-55671-227-2
ISSN: 1040-0850

Printed in the United States of America

All Rights Reserved

No part of this publication may be reproduced, stored in a retrieval system, or transmitted in any form or by any means—electronic, mechanical, photocopy, recording, or otherwise—without the express permission of the SIL International. However, short passages, generally understood to be within the limits of fair use, may be quoted without written permission.

Copies of this and other publications of the SIL International may be obtained from:

International Academic Bookstore
SIL International
7500 W. Camp Wisdom Road
Dallas, TX 75236-5699

Voice: 972-708-7404
Fax: 972-708-7363
Email: academic_books@sil.org
Internet: http://www.ethnologue.com

Contents

List of Maps viii
List of Figures viii
List of Tables. ix
Acknowledgements xi
1 Introduction 1
    1.1 The Gurage Cluster and Mesmes 1
    1.2 The Gurage language survey of 2001 2
    1.3 The Identification of the Lects in the Gurage Cluster 5
    1.4 Historical Work on the Gurage Varieties 7
        1.4.1 The Work of Leslau 7
        1.4.2 The Work of Hetzron 7
        1.4.3 A New Proposal for Ethio-Semitic Classification. . . 10
    1.5 The Debate over the Semitic Homeland 11
    1.6 Previous Research on Mesmes. 13
        1.6.1 The Work of Bender: The Wordlist,
        Lexicostatistics, and Grammatical Paradigms 13
        1.6.2 Hetzron on Mesmes 14
2 Establishing the Socio-Historical Context 17
    2.1 The Importance of the Social Setting 17
    2.2 The Gurage–Hadiyya Contact Situation 17
    2.3 The Recent History and Current Status of Mesmes 19
        2.3.1 An Interview with the Terminal Speaker 19
        2.3.2 The Shift to Hadiyya and the Death of Mesmes . . . 21
        2.3.3 The Maintenance of Identity Across
        Language Death. 23

3 The Implications of Language Death 27
   3.1 The Reliability Question 27
      3.1.1 The Challenge of a Terminal Speaker 27
   3.2 An Evaluation of the Reliability of the Mesmes Data . . . 28
      3.2.1 The Reliability of the Mesmes Wordlist 28
      3.2.2 The Reliability of the Mesmes Text 28
   3.3 Linguistic Implications 29
      3.3.1 Externally Induced Changes. 30
      3.3.2 Internally Induced Changes 30
      3.3.3 Reduction and Replacement Trends in
      Language Contact. 31
   3.4 The Modes of Language Death 32
   3.5 The "Later Loss" Hypothesis and "Rusty Speakers" 33
   3.6 An Examination of the Mesmes Text in Light of the
   Linguistic Implications 34
      3.6.1 Possible Examples of the Impact of Language
      Death in the Mesmes Text. 35
      3.6.2 Evidence of Maintenance of Inherited
      Structure in Mesmes 38

4 The Genetic Position of Mesmes 43
   4.1 The Establishment of Mesmes as a Gurage Language . . . 43
      4.1.1 The Ethnonym as Evidence of
      Guragoid Placement 43
      4.1.2 The Main Verb Marker Retention Attesting
      to a Genetic Link with Gurage 44
      4.1.3 Morpho-Syntactic Evidence of Guragoid
      Relationship 45
      4.1.4 Lexical Evidence of Close Relationship
      with PWG. 47
   4.2 Shared Innovations Linking Mesmes with PWG 48
      4.2.1 Innovations in the Pronominal Paradigm 49
      4.2.2 Markedness Reversal and the Beginnings
      of an Obstruent Chain Shift. 53
      4.2.3 An Examination of the Systematicity of
      Relative Chronology in the Mesmes Data 55
      4.2.4 Additional Links Between Mesmes and PWG 60
         4.2.4.1 Weakening of the Bilabial Nasal
         and the Genesis of the Non-Etymological /n/ . . . 60

   4.2.4.2 Relevant Vocalic Length 65
   4.2.4.3 Other Vocalic Changes in Mesmes 68
   4.2.4.4 Pharyngeal Archaisms and
      Systematic Metathesis 69
5 Evidence of Contact-Induced Change in the Mesmes Data. . 73
 5.1 The Nature of Externally-Induced Change. 73
 5.2 Loanwords in the Mesmes Wordlist 74
 5.3 Paradigmatic Leveling in Mesmes 75
 5.4 The Mesmes Final Vocalism. 76
 5.5 Vocalic Phenomena in Mesmes 79
 5.6 Possible Syntactic Change as a Result of Contact 80
 5.7 Cushitic *Stop-Attacks* in Endegeny and Mesmes 83
6 Conclusion 85
 6.1 Subgrouping Internal to PWG 85
 6.2 Unerscoring the Holistic Approach 89
Appendices
 A Peripheral West Gurage Wordlist Comparison
   with Mesmes 91
 B Mesmes, Hadiyya and Kambaata Comparison 103
 C The Mesmes Text 109
 D Notes on the Analysis of the Mesmes Text 115
 E Gurage language survey Map with Principal Towns. . . 135
References 137

List of Maps

1.1	The Gurage Area in Ethiopia	3
1.2	Map of Gurage Speech Varieties	5
1.3	de Chaurand's Map from Cohen (1931)	15
6.1	Geography and Sound Change	87

List of Figures

1.1	Hetzron's Classification of Ethio-Semitic	8
1.2	Hetzron's Classification of Outer South Ethiopic	9
6.1	Proposed Subgrouping for Peripheral West Gurage	88

List of Tables

1.1 Average Comprehension Test Scores from Gurage Survey	4
1.2 Comparison of Mesmes Lexicostatistics with Other Gurage Lects	14
2.1 Lects Involved in the Gurage Convergence Area	18
4.1 Mesmes and PWG Verbal Morphology Comparison	46
4.2 Lexemes Unique to Mesmes and PWG	47
4.3 Mesmes, PWG, and Cheha Pronominal Paradigms	49
4.4 The Sound Correspondence /x:h/ in the Pronominal Paradigm	50
4.5 The Sound Correspondence /xʲ:ʃ/ in the Pronominal Paradigm	50
4.6 The Sound Correspondence /t:d/ in the Pronominal Paradigm	51
4.7 The Sound Correspondence /t:d/ in 'house'	51
4.8 The Sound Correspondence /t:d/ in 'fire'	52
4.9 The Sound Correspondence /t:d/ in 'neck'	53
4.10 The Sound Correspondence /dd:t/ in 'to throw down'	54
4.11 The Sound Correspondence /bb:p/ in 'to skin'	55
4.12 Guragoid and Mesmes Forms for 'leaf'	56
4.13 The Relative Chronology as Evidenced in 'leaf'	57
4.14 Guragoid and Mesmes Forms for 'moon(light)'	59
4.15 The Relative Chronology as Evidenced in 'moon(light)'	59
4.16 Historical Derivation for Mesmes 'ashes'	61
4.17 Historical Derivation for Mesmes 'claw'	62
4.18 Historical Derivation for Mesmes 'bird'	64
4.19 Historical Derivation for Mesmes 'three'	66
4.20 Historical Derivation for Mesmes 'rain (n)'	66
4.21 Historical Derivation for Mesmes 'mountain'	67
4.22 Historical Derivation for Mesmes 'one'	67
4.23 Pharyngeal Archaism in 'to hear'	70
4.24 Pharyngeal Archaism in 'to eat'	71
4.25 Systematic Metathesis in Endegeny and Mesmes	72
5.1 Comparison of Mesmes and Hadiyya Pronominal Paradigms	75
5.2 Examination of Mesmes Final Vocalism	77
5.3 Results of Final Vowel Comparisons Between Mesmes, Hadiyya and Kambaata	78
5.4 Bound Possessives in Mesmes, Endegeny, and Ennemor Attaching to 'house'	81
5.5 Comparison of Mesmes and Hadiyya Bound Possessives	82
6.1 Sound Change at Relative Time-Depths	86

Acknowledgements

I am grateful to the late M. Lionel Bender for his kindness in sending me his Mesmes fieldnotes, completed in 1969, containing his Mesmes wordlist and unpublished grammatical paradigms. I am also grateful to Linda Jordan, who organized, scanned, and e-mailed some of my fieldnotes from Ethiopia; Hussein Mohammed, my friend and co-worker on the Gurage language survey; and my SIL Ethiopia colleagues who sponsored my linguistic research. Jerold Edmondson has been an encouragement and an inexhaustible source for new ideas, answering many questions and critiquing early drafts. I am grateful to Peter Unseth, who, from his vast experience and knowledge of Ethiopian languages, offered both his expertise, through many hours of informal chats, as well as the use of his considerable Ethiopian library. I also appreciate the valuable criticism and input of Donald Burquest and Ronny Meyer, who commented on earlier drafts. I want to express sincere thanks to George Huttar for his many comments, helping me to clarify much.

I am grateful to Colleen Ahland who assisted me in the fieldwork as well as in positing some of the initial sound correspondences for use in an earlier work (Ahland 2006). I appreciate Heyru Mohammed, an Ennemor Gurage, who has been both a help and a friend while I have been working on the Mesmes text. Many thanks are also due to Girma Getahun and Alemayehu Hailu who helped with finalizing the Amharic translation of the text. I would also like to acknowledge the many Gurage people I've worked with, too many to name here, who have given freely of their time, by no means the least of which is Abegaz, the terminal speaker of Mesmes, who shared both his language as well as his personal history. Finally, I am grateful to God for the grace to complete this work.

1

Introduction

1.1 The Gurage Cluster and Mesmes

The Gurage cluster of languages belongs to the Ethio-Semitic family, which in turn is part of Western South Semitic within the larger family, Afroasiatic (Faber 1997). Found in the highlands to the south and southwest of Addis Ababa, Ethiopia's capital, over one million speakers claim one of the Gurage languages as their mother tongue today (Ethiopian Census Records 1994). The cluster is comprised of no less than fourteen distinct speech varieties,[1] all of which are believed to be genetically related one to another (Hetzron 1972). While much study has been done on the Gurage languages over the past one hundred years, one group, the Mesmes, has escaped all but the most cursory attention.

The Mesmes are found within the borders of the Hadiyya (Highland East Cushitic) language area. They are geographically isolated from close contact with other Ethio-Semitic languages. Hetzron (1977) suggests that Mesmes is closely related to Endegeny, one variety of the West Gurage cluster of varieties, or "lects," within the Outer South Ethiopic family. However, Hetzron did not publish any data to back up his claim.

---

[1] It must be noted that I, in keeping with Hetzron's classification of Ethiopian-Semitic (1972:119), do not consider the so-called East Gurage languages of Silt'e, Zway, Wolane, etc. to be part of the Gurage cluster. Rather, the cluster may be said to include: Kistane (Soddo), Dobi (Gogot), Mesqan, Muher, Gumera, Ezha, Aklil, Desa, Cheha, Gura, Ennemor, Enner, Endegeny, and Gyeto. And, of course, Mesmes would be included here, historically as well.

Today, the Mesmes language is no longer spoken. The Mesmes people have shifted to speaking Hadiyya. One remaining Mesmes speaker, nevertheless, has in fact been found. Members of this speaker's community consider this man to be the terminal speaker of Mesmes. While at the time I interviewed him in 2001 he had not spoken the language in thirty years, his speech closely matched the only known Mesmes wordlist, gathered by Bender in 1969.

This work documents the placement of Mesmes within Gurage as part of the Peripheral West Gurage subgroup. New evidence of a close relationship between Endegeny and Mesmes is provided and an examination of the contact-induced changes that have taken place in Mesmes as a result of borrowing from Hadiyya is also undertaken.

1.2 The Gurage language survey of 2001

Between the months of April and November of 2001, I, along with Colleen Ahland and Hussein Mohammed, conducted linguistic and sociolinguistic field research in the Gurage region. The region stretches from just south of Welk'it'e in the west (8°17.68 N and 37°47.20 E) and Bui in the east (8°19.59 N and 38°33.03 E) to a few miles south of Dink'ulla in the east (7°52.15 N and 37°48.50 E) and Qabul in the west (7°52.58 N and 38°02.02 E). The entire area within these coordinate points is considered Gurage by the inhabitants. Map 1.1 shows the location of the Gurage area within Ethiopia. The Gurage cluster spans an area of southwestern Ethiopia about 150 kilometers in length and about 80 kilometers in width, at the widest part.

Map 1.1. The Gurage Area in Ethiopia

The Gurage language survey was conducted under the auspices of the Gurage Zone Education Bureau; their help, insight, and assistance are greatly appreciated. The primary purpose of the research was to discover centers of communication and their respective linguistic boundaries within the cluster. During the course of the research, the team conducted sociolinguistic interviews with groups of adults, collected wordlists, recorded and translated texts, and carried out comprehension testing.[2] A holistic approach including a careful analysis of sociolinguistic factors, genetic relationship, reported levels of translectal intelligibility by the speakers themselves, and actual comprehension scores on recorded text tests from the other varieties was used to group the cluster into communication centers (Ahland 2003). Table 1.1 provides the average comprehension test scores.

---

[2] For a detailed discussion of recorded text testing methodology, see Eugene Casad's Dialect Intelligibility Testing, 1974. The basic concept is to elucidate inherent intelligibility between speech varieties by testing speakers on natural texts recorded from the other areas in question. Speakers who have had substantial or repeated contact with those varieties whose texts they will be tested on are not included in the study.

Table 1.1. Average Comprehension Test Scores from the Gurage language survey

Test Points (Location where testing was conducted)

Reference Points (Text which was played)	CH	EZ	MU	GY	IN	GU	EN	MS	MQ	DO	KI
CH	90	88	85	86	67	89	63		48	39	30
EZ		97				87					
MU	74	73	93						71	73	53
GY				98	83		94		67		
IN	78			75	89	67	89				
GU		89			88	97					
EN				77	90		93				
MS							78				
MQ	92	90	97	86					92	89	63
DO			85						61	96	76
KI			54						65	90	98

The abbreviations are: CH = Cheha, EZ = Ezha, MU = Muher, GY = Gyeto, IN = Inor, GU = Gura, EN =Endegeny, MS = Mesmes, MQ = Mesqan, DO = Dobi/Gogot, KI = Kistane/Soddo (Ahland 2001). The shaded cells indicate hometown scores, where test subjects were scored on the text from their own area.

This language survey was meant to build upon the earlier work on intelligibility by Gutt (1977) who established comprehension boundaries between Silt'e, Cheha, and Kistane. Thus, the need to investigate the levels of inherent intelligibility among the other Gurage varieties remained.

The findings of the Gurage language survey are shown on map 1.2 (see appendix E for a more detailed map including the principal towns). Their relevance here is to aid in examining both the geographic and linguistic relationships between the speech varieties of the cluster as well as to help establish which Gurage speech varieties are most likely to be closely related to Mesmes linguistically.

Map 1.2. Map of Gurage Speech Varieties

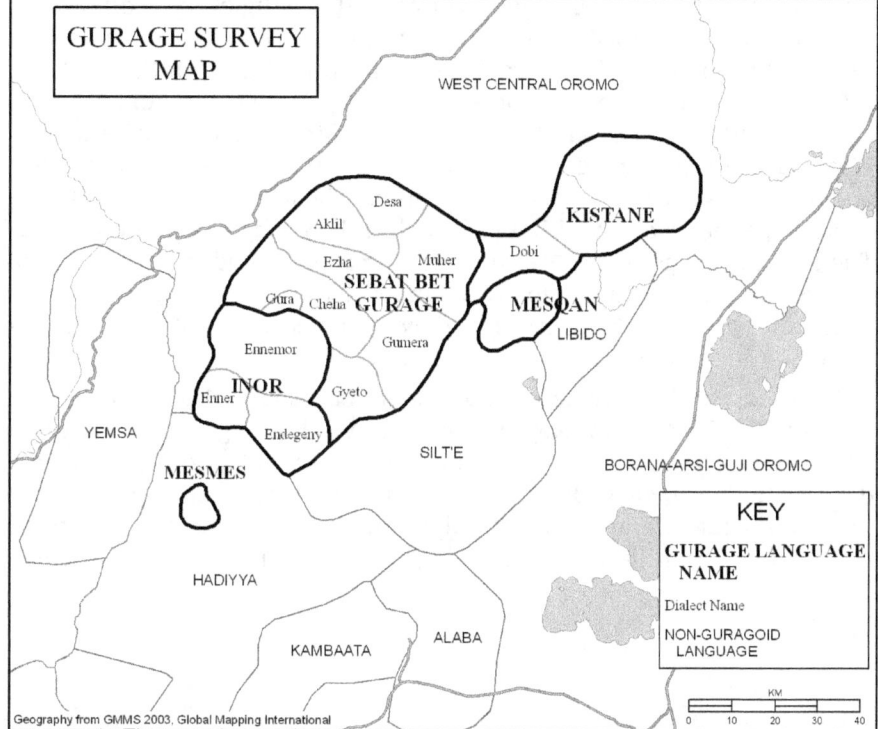

1.3 The Identification of the Lects[3] in the Gurage Cluster

The geographic areas of Gurage speech varieties are outlined in black in map 1.2. The names in all capital letters denote language groupings based on intelligibility findings, while the names in smaller font with initial capitals refer to the principal lects.

A quick overview of these lects will suffice for now. Within Kistane are found the Kistane and Dobi varieties.[4] Just south of Kistane is Mesqan. The western boundary of Dobi and Mesqan is the large Gurage mountain

---

[3] A lect as used here, refers to a speech variety characterized by a minimally distinctive set of phonological, morphological, and syntactic features. See 2.2.

[4] *Kistane* 'Christian' is the autoethnonym preferred by the speakers themselves. In most of the literature the group is called "Soddo," and its language "Soddinya." The local population considers Soddo to be the name of the geographic location, not the name of the people or the language. They refer to their language as *Kistaninya* 'the language of the Christians'.

range with elevations of nearly 10,000 feet. To the west of the mountains lies *Sebat Bet* 'Seven House' Gurage.[5] If intelligibility is allowed as a determiner of linguistic boundaries, Sebat Bet Gurage is comprised of Cheha (the center, both geographically and linguistically), Ezha, Muher (including the subdialects of Desa and Aklil), Gyeto, Gura, and Gumera. Finally, southwest of Sebat Bet lies the area of Inor, also called Peripheral West Gurage. Inor includes speakers of the Ennemor and Endegeny varieties as well as of the subdialect of Enner.[6] The area associated with the Mesmes people is outlined in black within the Hadiyya area in map 1.2. The northern edge of the Mesmes area is an estimated twenty-five kilometers from the southern tip of the Endegeny area. That is, the Mesmes community is completely surrounded by speakers of a non-Guragoid, non-Ethio-Semitic language.

According to the most recent Ethiopian Census (1994) published at the time of the Gurage language survey, the total Gurage population was 1.2 million. The population of the Mesmes community, however, was not documented, as people claiming Mesmes ethnicity had not been counted separately from Hadiyya. The Hadiyya population itself was said to be as high as one million with as many as 600,000 monolinguals (Census 1994).

---

[5] Today, the name *Sebat Bet* denotes a social network of peoples. The Gurage language survey research team and I have found the Muher (including Desa and Aklil), Ezha, Cheha, Gura, Gumera, Gyeto, and Ennemor peoples to be generally accepted as part of this social network. Historically speaking, the *Sebat Bet* 'Seven Houses' was a political alliance formed from the *Amist Bet* 'Five Houses' at some time after 1889 (Shack 1966:205). Shack adds, "There is a consensus of opinion that before 1875 the Chaha, Muher, Gyeto, Ennemor and Ezha tribes formed a tribal federation then known as Amist Bet." He notes the later addition of the Aklil and Wolane groups as the foundation of the seven houses, Sebat Bet. For purely linguistic reasons, Ennemor is not considered part of Sebat Bet in the present classification, despite its historic social link with Sebat Bet. Rather, Ennemor groups closely with Endegeny and Enner, forming the Peripheral West Gurage subgroup (Hetzron 1977). This Peripheral West Gurage subgroup is denoted as *Inor* in map 1.2. Gyeto, according to Hetzron and the Gurage language survey team's findings, is on the linguistic border between Sebat Bet and Inor. Thus, in terms of the classification proposed above, the Sebat Bet delineation follows social boundaries rather than linguistic ones. I have elected to use the name here because it is so widely known and accepted, even as a term referring to the language, though not necessarily referring to those groups which were a part of the historic Sebat Bet federation.

[6] The actual nature of Enner is unclear to me. The Gurage language survey team did not attempt to locate any speakers of Enner itself, but found that both Ennemor and Endegeny claim it as a sort of subdialect.

1.4 Historical Work on the Gurage Varieties

The Gurage cluster has long been the subject of linguistic inquiry. Some of the most prominent scholars to tackle the Ethio-Semitic languages have worked on these lects. In order to set the stage for understanding the internal subgrouping within Gurage and the placement of Mesmes in that group, the works of two researchers in particular figure greatly: Wolf Leslau and Robert Hetzron.

1.4.1 The work of Leslau

Leslau has worked on the Gurage lects for more than a half century. His research has produced a quantity of information unparalleled in the study of Ethio-Semitic languages. His three-volume *Etymological Dictionary of Gurage* (1979) is undoubtedly the single greatest contribution to the corpus of Gurage language data.

In addition to his lexicography mentioned above and numerous articles on the Gurage languages, Leslau has examined the historical relationship of the Gurage speech varieties, grouping within Gurage the varieties known as East Gurage (Silt'e, Wolane, and Zway). Leslau argues for a single parent to account for all these Gurage languages (1965, 1969). Others have dissented, the most prominent voice being that of Hetzron.

1.4.2 The work of Hetzron

Hetzron's work has built upon the foundation of Leslau and other linguists who have worked on the Gurage varieties, and he has clearly acknowledged his debt to previous pioneers, most principally Leslau. However, Hetzron himself was the first to use the historical-comparative approach to classify Gurage lects based on shared innovations. His *Ethiopian Semitic: Studies in Classification* (1972) outlines his findings for all of the Ethio-Semitic family. Later (1977) he published *The Gunnän Gurage Languages*, an in-depth analysis of the interrelatedness of the Gurage lects and their historical placement within the cluster based on shared innovations. It is in this work that Hetzron identifies problems with the earlier Gurage classifications.

The most significant problem attracting Hetzron's attention grows out of Leslau's classification, which was not based solely on shared innovations but also relied on "archaisms and phenomena attributable to Cushitic influence" (Hetzron 1977:21).[7] Because of Hetzron's rigorous application of the comparative method, only his classification of Gurage is referred to in this work. Unlike Leslau, Hetzron does not include the so-called East Gurage varieties within the same subgroup as other Gurage lects. Rather, East Gurage is positioned within Transversal South Ethiopic (1972:119). See Figures 1.1 and 1.2, based on Hetzron (1972:119) for Hetzron's classification of Ethio-Semitic in general and Outer South Ethiopic in particular.

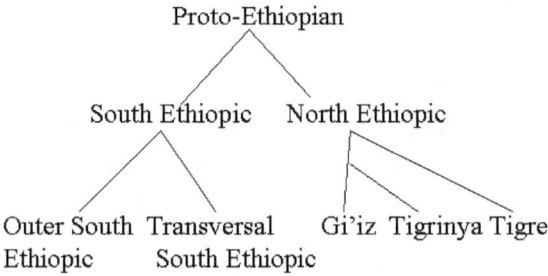

Figure 1.1. Hetzron's Classification of Ethio-Semitic.

Before continuing, it is necessary to consider a few of the more important subgroups shown in figures 1.1 and 1.2. Since the initial focus is to understand Gurage, as opposed to examining the broader Ethio-Semitic context, and then to consider the placement of Mesmes, attention must be centered on the classification of Outer South Ethiopic in figure 1.2.

The principal division between the n-group and the tt-group is based on an innovation Hetzron noted in the main verb markers, inherited from the earliest forms of Semitic (1977). These main verb markers originally signified indicative mood in Proto-Semitic. The "tt" form is an innovative shibboleth, opposed to the more archaic "n" form. Western Gurage has essentially lost these main verb markers, except for an isolated retention in Peripheral West Gurage where they have been maintained in the past form of the existential verb.

---

[7] See Hetzron (1977:21–22) for a complete synopsis of this debate.

1.4 Historical Work on the Gurage Varieties

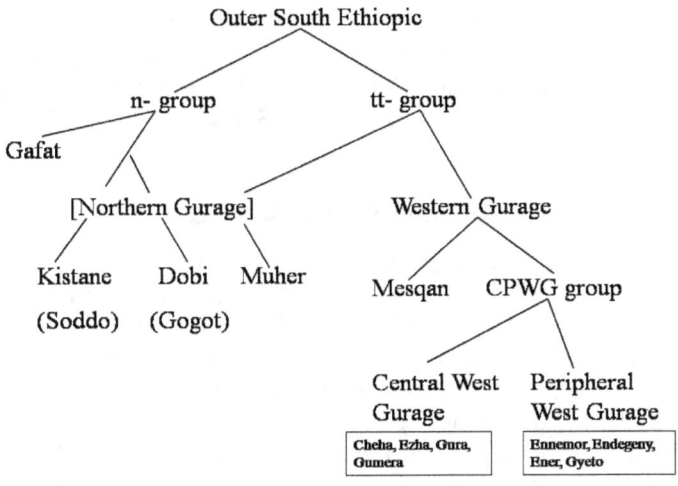

Figure 1.2. Hetzron's Classification of Outer South Ethiopic.

Hetzron (1972) positions Muher, a "tt" variety, with Soddo and Gogot into Northern Gurage, thus creating the image of two parents (both the "n" and "tt" groups) for this group. Hetzron's justification for this is that Muher, while clearly showing the "tt" innovation as well as other innovations found in Western Gurage varieties, also shares an innovation with Kistane and Dobi: the loss of /t/ in the third person singular independent pronouns (1972:121).[8]

Within Western Gurage is found the split between Mesqan and what Hetzron has called the CPWG group (1972:119). The development of this split is based on the innovation of two future tenses (definite and indefinite) in both the Central West and Peripheral West varieties, while Mesqan has preserved the more archaic system (Hetzron 1977:24). There are, of course, many other innovations that further confirm the genetic divisions into these lectal complexes. Some of the more interesting sound correspondences are dealt with in chapter 4.

---

[8] I believe the shared innovation with Kistane and Dobi is more likely due to contact phenomena than to actual shared history. The Muher speakers are in frequent contact with Dobi speakers in particular. This and the fact that Muher does share many more innovations with Western Gurage than this single innovation with Northern Gurage suggest that Muher belongs within Western Gurage but shows some external influence, most probably from Dobi.

Hetzron's Central West Gurage (CWG) includes Cheha, Ezha, Gura, and Gumera. His Peripheral West Gurage (PWG) includes Ennemor, Endegeny, Ener, and Gyeto.[9] For the most part (except for the distinctions covered in footnote 8), Hetzron's Northern Gurage corresponds to my Kistane; his Central West corresponds to my Sebat Bet; and his Peripheral West, to my Inor.

1.4.3 A new proposal for Ethio-Semitic classification

Girma Demeke (2001) argues for a classification differing from those proposed by Leslau and Hetzron. Working from the assumption that the Ethio-Semitic languages originated in Ethiopia at a time before Semitic speakers had left Africa and migrated to Asia,[10] he suggests that Ethio-Semitic is a daughter of Proto-Semitic and, moreover, a sister to the so-called Asian-Semitic languages (Girma 2001:64). His classification for Outer South Ethiopic also differs from Hetzron's. He classifies Muher as a Western Gurage language, while Ennemor, within Western Gurage (Hetzron's CPWG group) he classifies not with Endegeny as part of PWG but as part of CWG, closely related to Cheha (Girma 2001:78). It must be mentioned that the classification of Muher as a Western Gurage language corresponds nicely with the comprehension scores (table 1.1), the intelligibility reports, and the sociolinguistic information gathered during the Gurage language survey. But not all evidence confirms Girma's account: the classification of Ennemor as a CWG language is not supported by the survey results.

On this last point, it is to be noted that the classification of Ennemor is particularly important for understanding the place of Mesmes within Gurage. The findings of the Gurage language survey of 2001 show that Ennemor (labeled as Inor in table 1.1) speakers understood only 67 percent, on average, of the Cheha text. These same Ennemor speakers understood a full 90 percent of the Endegeny text. Also, in the Endegeny area,

---

[9] Note that there are some significant differences between Hetzron's genetic classification and the Gurage language survey team's intelligibility-based divisions. First, Hetzron classifies Muher as a Northern Gurage lect, more closely related to Dobi (Hetzron's Gogot) and Kistane (Hetzron's Soddo) than any of the Sebat Bet lects. Second, Hetzron places Gyeto in the Peripheral West Group. Hetzron does note Gyeto as a "special problem" in classification in that it also shares some features in common with Central West Gurage (1972). In the final analysis, Hetzron argues that Gyeto is essentially a PWG lect with "strong Cheha influence" (1972:71–73). The discussion in chapter 4 will show that Gyeto diverges early in the development of PWG and does not participate in a number of important PWG innovations.

[10] For discussion of this migration out of Africa and the Semitic homeland debate, see 1.5.

Endegeny speakers scored an average of 63 percent on the Cheha text and 89 percent on the Ennemor text. The results of the Gurage language survey's sociolinguistic questionnaires suggest that due to roads and shared markets Ennemor speakers have more contact with Cheha speakers than with Endegeny speakers.[11] This, taken in conjunction with the presence of regular sound correspondences linking Ennemor with the rest of PWG (discussed in chapter 4), provides strong evidence that Ennemor is a PWG language.

1.5 The Debate over the Semitic Homeland

Before any specific discussion of previous research on the Mesmes language can be undertaken, it is important to consider the wider debate regarding the origins of the Semitic languages. For many years it was argued that the Semitic presence in Ethiopia came as a result of migration to Ethiopia from southern Arabia and Yemen (Ullendorff 1960, Leslau 1968, Hetzron 1972). This well-accepted notion has been challenged by Murtonen's suggestion that the Ethiopian Semitic speakers must have separated from South Arabian Semitic far earlier than the proposed migrations in order for the vast diversity of lexicon, phonology, and grammar found today in extant Ethio-Semitic languages (Murtonen 1967) to have developed. Bender, in his "Upside-Down Afrasian" (1997), argues that on the basis of the linguistic evidence (grammatical isomorphs, syntactic phenomena, and lexical data), the Afroasiatic homeland, contra the "out-of-Asia" hypothesis, is likely in the Blue-White Nile confluence area near present-day Khartoum (Bender 1997:20). Semitic, Bender asserts, is "a relatively recent offshoot of the [Berber-Semitic-Cushitic] branch of Afrasian" (Bender 1997:25). Bender also notes the benefits gained by an "out-of-Africa" hypothesis for Semitic: the so-called "problem of diversity" within Ethio-Semitic languages vanishes (Bender 1997:27).

Hudson (2002) also suggests that since Afroasiatic is most thoroughly attested in Africa, with only the Semitic subfamily of its six subfamilies found in part of the continent, and since the most numerous Semitic group is Ethio-Semitic, it is likely that the earliest Semitic speakers were found in the area of present-day Ethiopia. He writes:

> Ethiopian Semitic speakers must reasonably be thought the autochthonous descendants of the first Semites, who have lived in Ethiopia alongside their Afroasiatic siblings and neighbors, the

---

[11] Thus, it is highly unlikely that high scores between Ennemor and Endegeny would be due to contact as opposed to inherent intelligibility.

> Cushitic and Omotic speakers, since in prehistoric times all three moved out of the Afroasiatic house... (Hudson 2002:1770)

Hudson employs the notion of linguistic diversity marking the homeland—meaning that the location where the greatest dialectal/linguistic variation is found may be suspected to be the *Urheimat* or original home. Also, he employs Hetzron's archaic heterogeneity argument: "When related languages are compared, the system that exhibits the most inner heterogeneity is likely to be the closest to the ancestor-system" (Hetzron 1976:89). Hudson offers examples of heterogeneity in the degree of structural difference among Ethio-Semitic languages (2002). Thus on both counts, Ethio-Semitic appears to be autochthonous in his view. First, he points out that Ethio-Semitic is the most diverse Semitic group with sixteen languages. And he further notes that on structural grounds, Ethio-Semitic is more heterogeneous in its subsystems, and thus provides reasonable means for reconstructing the proto-language. He does not suggest that one must rework all of Hetzron's tree for Ethio-Semitic:

> The Semitic proto-language arose in Ethiopia. After groups of these Semitic speakers separated and moved into Arabia and beyond, the Ethiopian Semites separated into northern and southern groups. Other separations of peoples and resulting evolution of languages in northern and southern Ethiopia may closely follow Hetzron's theory above (Hudson 2000:79)

That said, however, the Gurage languages, in particular, appear to share a significant number of archaisms that many have noticed. Before Murtonen's and Hudson's work, some of these archaic features were perhaps misconstrued to be the results of contact with Cushitic languages, and thus reflexes of an earlier Afroasiatic language, rather than retentions from Proto-Semitic. In light of Hudson's argument regarding the Ethiopian origin of the Semitic subfamily, these archaisms may need reconsideration:

> A number of features of Proto-Ethiopian and even Proto-Semitic have been traced in Gurage languages, such as items enumerated in Leslau (1951), the main verb markers identified in Leslau (1967) and Hetzron (1968), and archaic vowel of the jussive verb hypothesized in Leslau (1968a). The absence of these features in northern Ethiopian is of interest, particularly if Gurage is assumed to be derived from the northern languages, and thought to be in general more innovative under the influence of intimate contact with its close Cushitic neighbors (Hudson 1977:129)

Murtonen (1967) also suggests that the archaic features in Ethio-Semitic are the result of an autochthonous Semitic-speaking community in Ethiopia:

> Moreover, the archaic features of Tigre and Gurage can hardly be accounted for otherwise than on the supposition that they have been living apart from the rest of Ethiopic for long periods, and since ancient times, which hardly could have been the case, had they come together with other ancestors of present-day Ethiopians from South Arabia; Cushitic and Egyptian affinities also point to a permanent stay of most Ethiopians on the African continent (Murtonen 1967:74)

Despite this debate concerning the Semitic homeland and the possible status of Ethio-Semitic as an autochthonous group whose Gurage languages, in particular, may include some of the most archaic varieties, I have chosen to rely on the classification proposed by Hetzron on the grounds that it is the most extensive and careful comparative study as yet undertaken of the Gurage languages. It remains to be seen whether or not future research will demonstrate the need for further reorganization of the internal branching of Ethio-Semitic.

1.6 Previous Research on Mesmes

A discussion of the previous work related to Mesmes is now in order. Very little information was available on Mesmes when compared with what is known about the other languages in the area. Until my own work, Marvin Lionel Bender was the only linguist to have published Mesmes data.

1.6.1 The work of Bender: The wordlist, lexicostatistics, and grammatical paradigms

In 1969, Bender and Stinson, an expatriate missionary who assisted Bender in some of his work in the area, collected a ninety-nine-item wordlist from a Mesmes speaker in the area of Hosanna town in southwestern Ethiopia. The wordlist was published along with a large lexicostatistic comparison of various languages in Ethiopia in *The Journal of Anthropological Linguistics* in 1971. Bender's findings regarding the lexicostatistic comparison of Mesmes with other lects in the area is summarized in table 1.2.

Note that Mesmes is most "similar" to Ennemor. Bender's work, which predates Hetzron's comparative work, does in fact agree with Hetzron's findings. However, it must be noted that while lexicostatistics does show lexical similarity between lects, it cannot be taken as a completely reliable method to determine genetic relationships, as its similarity matrices do not cull out borrowings or retentions—neither of which can be used to show any specific shared history.

Table 1.2. Comparison of Mesmes Lexicostatistics with Other Gurage Lects

Cheha				
80	Mesqan			
89	76	Gyeto		
81	70	83	Ennemor	
56	58	59	68	Mesmes

The importance of Bender's Mesmes wordlist should not be underestimated, however. Currently, his ninety-nine-item list is still the main corpus available on the lect. In addition to the wordlist, Bender and Stinson collected a few grammatical paradigms showing the pronoun set, the bound possessives, and the conjugations of two verb forms. These grammatical paradigms were never published.

1.6.2 Hetzron on Mesmes

As has already been mentioned, Hetzron is credited with the most comprehensive study of Gurage based on shared innovations. While Bender and Stinson's grammatical paradigms were never published, it does appear that Hetzron did see these data and was able to make a general observation:

> M. L. Bender…mentioned the existence of a Gurage group, called Mesmes (*məsməs*, probably a nickname based on the vocatively used word *məs* 'man') outside of Gurageland proper, in Bushana, west of Hossana….On the basis of a 99-word-list and a handful of grammatical items provided by Bender, the present writer has been able to identify it as a dialect of Endegeñ. (Hetzron 1977:4)

Apart from a number of references to Hetzron's statement above, there is very little mention of the Mesmes language in the linguistic literature.

1.6 Previous Research on Mesmes

In the remainder of his Gurage treatise, Hetzron does not deal with Mesmes at all. He does not include any evidence from Bender's list or from his grammatical paradigms to back up his claims.

In the same work, however, Hetzron does mention a map by de Chaurand containing a reference to a Masmasa group in the vicinity of Gurage. The map (see map 1.3) is dated 1894 and has been reproduced in Cohen (1931:69). Masmasa is placed between the Alaba and Kambaata groups, a significant distance southeast of where the Mesmes are found today.

Map 1.3. de Chaurand's 1894 map identifying Masmasa; from Cohen (1931)

It is unclear if this *Masmasa* is closely connected to the *Mesmes* or if they belong to another Ethio-Semitic-speaking people who have since moved from the area. The supposition that the Mesmes once lived closer to the Kambaata than they do today is strengthened by the presence of a number of Kambaata loanwords in the Mesmes data.

In Bender's original fieldnotes from 1969, he recorded that his Mesmes informant claimed heritage from the Oyatta, a kingly clan of the

Kambaata. Dirk Bustorf (personal communication, 2003) has mentioned that the oral tradition of the Kambaata asserts that the early ancestors of Kambaata and Mesmes were brothers, together with Donga, Kauka/ Dawro, Loka, Bosha, and Yemsa. Linguistically speaking, this appears quite unlikely since the myth involves genetic links between Cushitic-, Ethio-Semitic-, and Omotic-speaking peoples.[12]

The most recent mention of Mesmes in the literature is found in Sim's (1989) doctoral dissertation on Hadiyya, in which a small Guragoid community called Masmas is identified as "declining": "There is also the small, and now declining Masmas (Gurage) community in Konteb Woreda." (1989:4) The Konteb Woreda includes the area around the town of Morsito near where the Mesmes are found today. Nothing more is mentioned regarding the Mesmes people or their speech form in Sim's work. It is unclear how Sim deduced that the Mesmes were declining in the mid-1980s when he surveyed the Hadiyya area. His insight, however, does certainly correspond to the proposed recent history of Mesmes I propose in more detail in chapter 2.

This work attempts to evaluate Hetzron's claim of close relationship between Mesmes and Endegeny, through an examination of Bender's data, both his wordlist and his previously unpublished grammatical data, as well as through additional data gleaned from my Mesmes text. It is shown that Mesmes is a PWG language and has shared history with Ennemor and Endegeny in particular. The comparative analysis is undertaken in chapter 4.

---

[12] Of course, genetic lineage and linguistic inheritance need not follow the same route; groups may be genetically related without sharing linguistic relatedness.

2
Establishing the Socio-Historical Context

2.1 The Importance of the Social Setting

Languages do not exist within a vacuum. They are not "protected" from the influences of other languages or the desires of their own speakers. Any study of historical linguistics must, at the very least, consider the social context and its possible effects on the linguistic changes that have occurred. Thomason and Kaufman (1988:4) write:

> The key to our approach...is that the history of a language is a function of the history of its speakers, and not an independent phenomenon that can be thoroughly studied without reference to the social context in which it is embedded.

Indeed, the social context is a particularly important means for understanding some of the changes found in Mesmes. Therefore, before undertaking an examination of the data, the setting and social history must first be established.

2.2 The Gurage–Hadiyya Contact Situation

Leslau was the first to recognize the significance of the contact situation between the Gurage languages and the Cushitic languages (1945, 1959, 1992e). These early accounts of contact led to the application of the term

Sprachbund to this geographic area. A number of other scholars have since developed greater interest in the Gurage-Cushitic convergence area. More recent works have included Ferguson (1976) and Zaborski (1991).

The term *convergence* has come to be associated with the established phenomenon whereby speech varieties in close geographical proximity whose speakers share a high degree of multilectalism may "converge," becoming more like one another through the minimalization of differences among those varieties, or lects. I have chosen the term *lect* over *language* to cover the convergence process that occurs between even very closely related linguistic varieties, which is often the case in this linguistic area.

Those lects generally accepted as participating in the Gurage convergence area are listed in table 2.1.

Table 2.1. Lects Involved in the Gurage Convergence Area

HIGHLAND EAST CUSHITIC	EASTERN GURAGE	WESTERN GURAGE	NORTHERN GURAGE
Maraqo/Libido	Silt'e	Mesqan	Muher
Alaba	Wolbareg	Ennemor	Dobi
Hadiyya	Wolane	Endegeny	
Qabena			

There is, of course, some debate about which speech varieties have close enough contact to be considered part of this convergence area; only the varieties I know from personal experience, from personal communication from other researchers, or from the existing literature to have been undergoing some contact-induced changes likely attributable to convergence have been included in table 2.1.

For the purposes of this work, only the interplay of the Peripheral West Gurage lects (Ennemor, Endegeny, etc.) and Hadiyya is of concern. The other lects, while they play a part in the general convergence within the area, are not immediately involved here, because the speakers of Peripheral West Gurage lects do not know the other lects involved, though many do in fact speak Hadiyya, and many Hadiyya speak the Peripheral West Gurage lects as well.

Since the most salient focus in this work is to show the genetic relationship between Mesmes and Peripheral West Gurage, concern is centered not on changes in the Hadiyya language as a result of contact with Gurage languages, but on the effects of Hadiyya on Gurage.

2.3 The Recent History and Current Status of Mesmes

In May of 2001, I, along with Colleen Ahland, Hussein Mohammed, and Ralph Siebert, traveled to the Boshana area of Ethiopia in search of Mesmes speakers. The trip was made in conjunction with the intelligibility survey mentioned previously. Before setting out, I conferred with several colleagues both at the Linguistics Department at Addis Ababa University (AAU) and at the Ethiopian Language Research Center (የኢትዮጵያ ቋንቋ ጥናትና መርመር ማዕከል) concerning the location(s) where the Mesmes people might be found. The area outside of the town of Morsito within the general region of Boshana was suggested as a good place to begin. However, the general reaction among linguists at AAU was that we would likely not find any speakers of Mesmes. The word at the University was that the language had become extinct—an assumption which turned out to be essentially correct.

A German missionary living in the town of Hosanna had also suggested that we visit the village of Homacho, west of Morsito. He had heard of Mesmes people living in that area. Today, the Mesmes people can be found by a roughly twenty-five-kilometer, four-hour drive (by 4-wheel-drive vehicle) west of Homacho, in the K'ebele (a small political unit, below the level of a county) known as Ast'ey.

2.3.1 An interview with the terminal speaker

The ethnic group living in this area refer to themselves as Mesmes. The research team found rather quickly that none of the Mesmes people living in Ast'ey were able to speak Mesmes. The inhabitants claimed that they normally speak Hadiyya and sometimes some Oromo (Cushitic) and Amharic (Ethio-Semitic), a claim very much in agreement with what linguists at AAU had suggested. But the Mesmes of Ast'ey did, in fact, know of one elderly man who could still speak Mesmes, and two of them volunteered to guide us to his home. The journey required a thirty-minute hike from Ast'ey.

This elderly speaker of Mesmes, here referred to by the pseudonym Abegaz,[1] lives about a mile south of Hok'e village. As far as those in his community are concerned, he is the last-known speaker of the Mesmes language. Abegaz was unsure of his age, but on the basis of his marriage during the Italian occupation of Ethiopia under Mussolini, I estimate his age to have been roughly 80 years in 2001. He was born in Ast'ey and lived his whole life in that area. Mesmes was his first language. He spoke the Mesmes language with his parents, siblings, and most of his friends.

Abegaz said his father was Mesmes but his mother was Endegeny. She was from the village of Buch'a, about a day's journey from Ast'ey. He said that his mother spoke Mesmes, which she considered to be the same language as Endegeny, her native tongue. He learned to speak Hadiyya while growing up. Some of his older childhood friends were Hadiyya, and this second language quickly became his primary language outside his home as he came of age. Abegaz could not give a specific time frame, but did say that he was "older" when he learned to speak Hadiyya. He was a Hadiyya speaker by the time he married. It therefore seems likely that he had learned Hadiyya in his early to mid teens.

Interestingly enough, Abegaz's parents were not Hadiyya speakers. It appears that Mesmes children of Abegaz's generation were not all learning Hadiyya from their parents or their other earliest contacts, but acquiring it as a second language.

In the 1940s, Abegaz married a Hadiyya girl who could not speak Mesmes. They lived in Ast'ey, where he worked as a farmer. They raised their children speaking only Hadiyya. His children never learned to speak Mesmes. Of an advanced age when I met him, Abegaz had outlived all his agemates. He was able to continue speaking Mesmes with his brother, until his brother's death in the 1970s.

When Bender and Stinson collected the Mesmes wordlist in 1969, linguists were unaware that speakers of Mesmes were in the process of losing their language (Bender, personal communication, 2003). Their informant made no mention of the Mesmes' shift to the Hadiyya language. However, based on information gathered during our interview with the terminal speaker and on the lack of Mesmes speakers today, it does seem that Mesmes was moribund well before 1969. While Abegaz and his age-cohorts spoke Mesmes, they must have learned Hadiyya as a second language; that their generation did not pass Mesmes on to their children suggests that normal transmission of the language must have stopped

---

[1] The pseudonym *Abegaz* is an Amharic military title, 'the father of the battle', bestowed upon many in the Gurage area.

2.3 The Recent History and Current Status of Mesmes

in the 1950s at the latest, and possibly earlier. Since life expectancy in Ethiopia averages only around 47 years, the lack of speakers today has a very natural account.

Dirk Bustorf, an anthropologist who has conducted research on the inter-ethnic relations between Leemo-Hadiyya and Endegeny, has interviewed a number of people who are ethnically Mesmes and live outside of Boshana proper. He found no speakers of the Mesmes language and was told by his informants that their language had disappeared with the previous generation (Bustorf, personal communication, 2003).

2.3.2 The shift to Hadiyya and the death of Mesmes

Wurm notes that language death as a result of shift can often be tied to a variety of influences that affect the attitude of speakers toward their own language:

> Broadly speaking, such situations tend to occur if a speech community comes into economic, cultural or political contact with another community or population speaking a different language and which is economically stronger and more advanced than the first speech community, or culturally aggressive, or politically more powerful and mighty (Wurm 1991:5)

With these possible influences in mind, it is not difficult to imagine what prompted the shift to Hadiyya. First, the Mesmes, as an Ethio-Semitic speaking people, must have migrated to the area from the north. It is assumed, from the relationship with the Gurage languages, that the Mesmes were at one time living in contact with other Gurage groups. An alternative account could be, of course, that Hadiyya-speaking peoples spread north, surrounding and isolating the Mesmes and eventually cutting them off entirely from the rest of Gurage. Abegaz and other Mesmes people in Ast'ey, however, told the research team that the Mesmes had been the ones to come down from the north. Yet interestingly enough, Abegaz did not include Mesmes as part of the Gurage southern migration. Rather, he simply said they came from Gonder, the home of the old, northern kingdom and important seat of Ethio-Semitic culture. This separate account of the genesis of the Mesmes people is undoubtedly encouraged among the people because it relates to noble beginnings and a prestigious lineage. Regardless of whether the Mesmes migrated south or whether the Hadiyya spread to the north, the fact remains: the Mesmes were separated from other Ethio-Semitic language communities.

In addition to isolation, the status of Hadiyya must have played a crucial role in the demise of the Mesmes language. According to the 1994 Ethiopian Census records, there are about one million mother-tongue speakers of Hadiyya, nearly 600,000 of whom are monolinguals. The proportion of monolinguals would have been even higher fifty or one hundred years ago. If the Mesmes, who like all Gurage are known as traders, wished to trade or conduct any commerce in the region, they would have had to learn Hadiyya. Cooper and Carpenter, writing on trade and language use in Ethiopian markets, comment:

> Thus, instead of the buyer and seller typically interacting in a common first language or in a common second language, it is likely that the seller typically accommodated himself to the buyer by speaking the buyer's first language. In the linguistically diverse contexts of these Ethiopian markets, therefore, it appears that transactions were facilitated by the multilingualism of the traders rather than by the emergence of a trade lingua franca (1976:254)

The fact that Abegaz's father did not speak Hadiyya is rather interesting. Of course, one cannot draw any significant conclusions based on this small bit of information, but, at least, this raises the possibility that the isolation of Mesmes from Gurage (whether by migration or the spread of Hadiyya) might have occurred as late as one hundred years ago. This scenario would help to explain why Abegaz's father did not speak Hadiyya. His mother, as mentioned earlier, was from Endegeny, so it is not likely that she had been exposed to the same degree of contact with Hadiyya speakers. She would have likely had some contact with Hadiyya speakers, but maybe not enough to prompt her to learn the language.

In addition to the above-mentioned factors of migration, relative population, and monolingualism, there are other influences that helped to secure Hadiyya in a position of prestige over Mesmes. Brenzinger, Heine, and Sommer note that languages that are spoken in urban areas are associated with world religions and are used as media of education are generally seen as prestigious vis-à-vis languages that are spoken in primarily rural areas, are associated with traditional religions, and are not used as media of instruction (1991:38). By each of these variables, Hadiyya would outrank Mesmes in terms of prestige. First, the large town of Hosanna is regarded as a center of Hadiyya language and culture for the entire area. Nowadays, the Mesmes still live to the west of Hosanna but are known to travel to market there occasionally. Second, while the Hadiyya people are associated with Ethiopian Orthodox and Protestant forms of Christianity,

2.3 The Recent History and Current Status of Mesmes

the Mesmes are primarily religious traditionalists, according to Bustorf, who has researched the traditional religion of the Endegeny and Mesmes peoples (personal communication, 2003). Third, and while far too recent to have caused the shift to Hadiyya, the Hadiyya language today is a standardized, written language used as a medium of instruction in area schools. The literacy rate in Hadiyya is estimated to be as high as 30–40 percent, according to Annika Utriainen, a literacy specialist working in the area (personal communication, 2004). For each of these reasons, Hadiyya would likely exert pressure on speakers of minority languages. These pressures, in turn, may affect language attitudes and language use patterns. This can lead to language shift and, in extreme cases, language death.

Brenzinger and Dimmendaal argue that language shift becomes language death once there is no longer any speech community using the language (1992:a3). Sasse defines the death of a language as the "cessation of regular communication in the language" (1992:18). Sasse's definition leaves room for the ritualistic use of the language in religious ceremonies, cultural celebrations, funerals, etc. I have found no evidence that the language had been maintained even in this "ritualistic" domain. In fact, the most basic vocabulary,[2] which is, at times, the last vestige of a dying language, appears to have been lost to all Mesmes people except the terminal speaker. During the checking of the Bender and Stinson wordlist, it became apparent that only Abegaz himself knew the words. The others in the group were shocked to find that our research team, including two foreigners, knew more about their lost language than they, the Mesmes people, did themselves.

2.3.3 The maintenance of identity across language death

Bustorf, in his research on the traditional religion(s) of the area surrounding Mesmes, did not find any evidence of the maintenance of the Mesmes language in any of the ceremonies (personal communication, 2003). The unsuccessful search by the Gurage survey research team and myself, as well as the testimony of Ethiopian linguists at AAU and Bustorf's anthropological work, are in complete agreement: by all accounts, Mesmes has died.

It has been argued that language is the most salient symbol of ethnicity (Fishman 1989). While this is undoubtedly often the case, research

---

[2] I take the notion of "basic vocabulary" to refer to those terms which are likely to be present in any language due to functional necessity (i.e., the domain of the home, the natural world, or some relationship to the human body, etc.).

on endangered languages is beginning to show that the situation is less predictable:

> ...the literature on language contact today reflects this relation [between language and ethnicity] more carefully and it is generally accepted that while linguistic, ethnic and culture boundaries tend to coincide in many cases, this is by no means a must (Brenzinger, Heine, and Sommer 1991:35)

It is this latter, less-isomorphic relationship between language and identity that characterizes the Mesmes situation. While the Mesmes have indeed lost their language, they have still maintained their ethnicity. First, they have continued to call themselves by their Guragoid ethnonym: /mɨsmɨs/, a reduplication of /mɨs/, meaning 'man'. This name is recognized by insiders as well as outsiders to the Mesmes community. Second, as previously mentioned, the Mesmes have preserved their "northern" migration myth of origin, linking themselves with their Semitic-speaking history. Their house construction, as well, sets the Mesmes apart from their Hadiyya neighbors. Like Gurage houses, the Mesmes houses in Ast'ey are made of split bamboo, woven through wooden poles. Naigzy, in his description of Ethiopian housing types, notes, "Generally, very little chika [mud] plaster is used in Gurage houses, and then only on the inside surface" (1971:116).[3] The Hadiyya houses in the area surrounding Ast'ey, on the other hand, are externally covered with a plaster of mud containing decorative paintings. Third, as late as 1991, the Mesmes had registered a political organization with the United Nations Disaster Preparedness Committee (UNDPC). Bahirwork Mesmes Nationals Unity Organization was registered on October 27, 1991 (http://www.africa.upenn.edu/eue_web/soup_may.htm). I was unable to find any information as to whether or not this is still an active organization today. At the very least, however, such concrete evidence does show that at least some of the Mesmes people are continuing to view themselves as distinct from Hadiyya.

That some Mesmes still cling to their Mesmes identity is particularly interesting given that ethnolinguistic minorities are often led to internalize negative images of themselves which have been imposed by the more dominant surrounding group. Dressler and Wodak-Leodolter point out, "...members of the minority may experience identity conflicts and disturbances so that they may avoid admitting their group membership and be afraid of negative stereotypes and prejudices" (1977:6). This is simply not

---

[3] Naigzy also notes that Gurage houses are distinct from other housing types in their uniformity: "All Gurage houses look remarkably alike...[the] details are treated with a uniformity that is unique among Ethiopian traditional house-types" (1971:115).

2.3 The Recent History and Current Status of Mesmes

the case with the Mesmes. Rather, the lack of negative in-group image is likely indicative of the lack of social and linguistic repression by the Hadiyya speakers.

Based on my experience in trying to locate the Mesmes, it can be argued that the Hadiyya people also see the Mesmes as distinct but not in any overtly negative sense. It can be assumed that on the basis of very frequent intermarriage practices the Hadiyya do not wish to keep the Mesmes separate. That is to say, presumably, the Mesmes could be absorbed into Hadiyya, if they wished. Nevertheless, at this point, it is clear the Mesmes remain a distinct ethnicity while having completely shifted to Hadiyya as their first language.

3

The Implications of Language Death

3.1 The Reliability Question

In recent years, the topics of language death and of endangered languages in general have received a great deal of attention. One of the most important considerations when examining a moribund or dying language is the reliability of the data. The smaller the speaking community, the more difficult it is to evaluate data which have been gathered (Dorian 1977).

3.1.1 The challenge of a terminal speaker

Dorian argues that even in the most difficult situation, "An isolated last speaker may betray the uncertainty of his productions by the manner of delivery" (1977:23). Beyond the evidence of halted speech is the general assumption that "reduction in use" results in "reduction in form" (Dorian 1977:24). Thus, it can be argued that terminal speakers offer only glimpses of what their language was like before the "reduction" and death set in. In short, data collected in situations where only one speaker can be found must not be considered completely representative of the language in its healthier days.

This does not mean that data collected from terminal speakers are of no value. The problem arises in assuming that the language of terminal speakers is representative of the language as it was when spoken by an entire community in many domains.

3.2 An Evaluation of the Reliability of the Mesmes Data

The Mesmes situation is characteristic of the "isolated last speaker" situation described above. As mentioned in chapter 2, only a single speaker of Mesmes could be found in the area. It is important to recall that this terminal speaker had not used the language in an estimated thirty years, since his brother's death.

3.2.1 The reliability of the Mesmes wordlist

Bender and Stinson's wordlist, collected in 1969, offers some corroborating evidence which aids in evaluating the Mesmes data. A comparison between the 1969 list and the speech of the terminal speaker, Abegaz, shows no significant change. It may be in this instance that the most basic vocabulary has been maintained due to the final domain of use having been that of the home and family (The reader will recall that the terminal speaker last spoke Mesmes with his brother.) It has been found in some cases that isolated lexical items are the last vestiges of a language which is dying (Dressler 1991).

While lexicons do undergo reduction, grammatical systems do so on an even greater scale. Dressler's final category beyond the "terminal speaker" is the "rememberer" who recalls "only isolated items" (Dressler 1991:99). In these cases, the grammar has been lost. It is no longer reconstructible in the mind of the speaker, although the lexicon may still be useful for comparative and reconstructive purposes. Such grammar loss could be expected to be the case with the Mesmes wordlist, but as is shown below, even much of the Mesmes grammar remains surprisingly intact.

3.2.2 The reliability of the Mesmes text

Unfortunately, there is no other recorded text of the Mesmes language than the one collected during the 2001 survey and presented and analyzed here and thus, no opportunity for comparison to help in evaluating the degree of reduction and reliability of the data. It is possible, however, to examine internal evidence to determine whether or not the terminal speaker's language has undergone some of the consequences of atrophy. During the recording of the text, there were frequent pauses as well as occasional reiterations, suggesting some degree of reduced fluency. The presence of some surprising Amharic loanwords like /nɛbbɛr/, an Amharic existential, must be mentioned. This loan is sprinkled throughout the text, despite the fact that the speaker also frequently uses the Guragoid existential with the PWG main verb marker /-d/: /banɛ-d/.

Despite the presence of a few loanwords and some reduced speaking fluency, it is remarkable how much in the text is indeed Guragoid. Endegeny speakers, when tested for comprehension of the Mesmes text with ten questions covering a range of syntactic and semantic categories, averaged a score of 78 percent.[1] This is significant since it is extremely unlikely that any of the test subjects in the Endegeny area had actually heard Mesmes spoken before: all of the testing was conducted in Dink'ulla, a principal Endegeny town, and all of the test participants were under age 40. Thus, it is likely that they were born after normal transmission of Mesmes had stopped.

The 78 percent comprehension score appears to be indicative of the relationship between Mesmes and Endegeny. During a post-test interview, when the subjects were asked individually to identify the language of the text, three commented that it was "old Endegeny." One of the older subjects claimed that this language was similar to "the language of my grandparents." Thus, it must be admitted that the Mesmes language as represented in the text has retained enough of its Peripheral West Guragoid inheritance to be at least recognizable to Endegeny speakers as a closely related language. None of the test participants indicated that the text language was "mixed" or "poor language." While it can be assumed that the Mesmes text probably contains some simplifications of earlier systems which would presumably have been found in the language in previous generations, the lexemes themselves, as well as the morphological marking and syntactic constructions, do offer insight into the genetic history of the language.

3.3 Linguistic Implications

Two overarching processes affect linguistic structures undergoing a process of language death. The first is the change brought about by interference from the second language into the first (Seliger and Vago 1991). The second process of change is internally motivated linguistic change where systems within a language simplify and regularize.

---

[1] This testing was in conjunction with the large-scale intelligibility survey of 2001 referred to in chapter 1 as the Gurage language survey.

3.3.1 Externally induced changes

Externally induced changes are brought about through a process of interlinguistic analogy where re-patterning of the first language takes place on the model of the second. It is commonly argued that these re-patternings may include everything from additions and other changes to the lexicon to changes in word order, semantics, agreement and case marking, and the use of calquing or loan translations where phrases and expressions from the second language are literally, and often ungrammatically, translated directly into the first language (Thomason and Kaufman 1988, Seliger and Vago 1991). In large-scale language shift, where a community as a whole is adopting a new language and using their first language in fewer and fewer domains, these external changes can often be expected.[2]

3.3.2 Internally induced changes

In addition to these externally induced changes, there are also internally motivated changes involving the reduction of marked forms to less marked forms (Seliger and Vago 1991). In many cases, analogical leveling works to eliminate irregular patterns and marked features, leading toward simplification and an increase in regularity. The reduction of allomorphy within paradigms is a natural result of such processes (Maher 1991). In extreme cases, where language death is imminent, loss of verbal morphology and decay in both inflectional and tense/aspect systems are found (Seliger and Vago 1991).

It is not assumed that language reduction progresses systematically from lexicon to phonology to morphology and then finally to syntax. Dressler and Wodak-Leodolter argue against "universal implications among parts of grammar as to their susceptibility to alloglottic influences" (1977a:9). However, there are implications for each of the linguistic subsystems with the overall trend being one of simplification.

The internal process of reduction itself, in addition to being an indication of death, is also a catalyst for linguistic death since heavily simplified systems are less likely to be preserved overall (Dressler and Wodak-Leodolter 1977a). Beyond paradigmatic and analogical leveling, even discourse styles undergo simplification.[3] Dressler and Wodak-Leodolter point

---

[2] Externally induced changes will be dealt with further in chapter 5.

[3] The topic of the Mesmes text certainly belongs to one of the speaker's domains most likely to be retained, even given the reduction of communicative situation that Abegaz was constrained by as an adult. That is, it can be assumed that he would have likely talked of his father with his brother and that a discussion of past events involving their own family

3.3 Linguistic Implications

out that stylistically speaking, the trend is toward the most casual speech style remaining in the end (1977b:37). The trend is toward "monostylism." Maher concurs:

> As language A dies out, speakers use it in fewer and fewer sociolinguistic contexts; it is suggested, therefore, that the need for stylistic variants in language A is reduced. Moreover, among intimates, context predetermines much of the message. The need for more formal, elaborated or context-independent speech varieties is, therefore, limited. It is supposed that elaborate language forms gradually die out, leaving only those informal variants used in the intimate setting. (Maher 1991:80)

3.3.3 Reduction and replacement trends in language contact

Julianne Maher, in her study of enclave speech communities (1991), notes that a community which is isolated from other speakers of its language and is surrounded by another more dominant language which the community members also speak undergoes similar restructuring, regardless of the group's particular history as a "transplant" immigrant community or as an "indigenous" community which has been surrounded by the more dominant group. In addition to the tendency toward simplification and reduction, enclave communities show a preference for periphrastic constructions and analytic forms over synthetic forms. Coordination, also, is preferred to embedded constructions. She writes, "Enclave languages rely on coordinating elements, simple juxtaposition, and contextual clues to express complex syntactic relations and to avoid embedded constructions" (Maher 1991:75). Finally, the loss of inflectional morphology often results in less flexible word order (Maher 1991:68).

The importance of Maher's study in the Mesmes context is that Mesmes must be considered an enclave speech community. As mentioned above, the Mesmes people are surrounded on all sides by the more dominant Hadiyya-speaking community. It is unclear, however, if the Mesmes are a transplanted Gurage community which has moved into Hadiyya territory, a remnant of a wider Gurage area which has since been cut off by northern movement of the Hadiyya, or a pioneer community whose base area later submerged. In all cases, Maher notes, the effects on the speech of enclave communities are very similar.

---

would have been part of the repertoire. Thus, it is not possible to use the Mesmes text to gauge the degree to which stylistic simplification has occurred.

3.4 The Modes of Language Death

Understanding the effects of death on a language requires knowledge of the dying process of the particular language in question. Campbell and Muntzel (1989) identify four basic types or modes of death: sudden, radical, gradual, and bottom-to-top. They note that most cases of language death discussed in the linguistic literature involve gradual death, where the language is lost through a slow shift toward the dominant language spoken in the area:

> This situation is characterized by a proficiency continuum determined principally by age (but also by attitude and other factors). Younger generations have greater proficiency in the dominant language and learn the obsolescing language imperfectly, if at all (Campbell and Muntzel 1989:185)

The nature of the contact and convergence between Mesmes and Hadiyya is certainly characteristic of the sort of situation where gradual death might be expected. The Mesmes have indeed shifted to speaking the more dominant Hadiyya language. Yet, as was mentioned in chapter 2, no semi-speakers of Mesmes were found. In fact, the Gurage survey team was unable to find even those Mesmes who could understand but not speak the language. This is perplexing, considering all examples of gradual death in the literature lead naturally to the existence of semi-speakers.

Campbell and Muntzel's account of radical death may shed light on the history of Mesmes. Radical death is rapid loss that is "usually due to severe political repression, often with genocide, to the extent that speakers stop speaking the language out of selfdefense, a survival strategy" (1989:183). The apparent peaceful intermarriage of Mesmes and Hadiyya people, the maintenance of the Mesmes ethnic identity, and the lack of any evidence of past political or ethnic conflict between the Mesmes and Hadiyya pose a challenge to the radical death hypothesis with regard to Mesmes. Yet the effects of radical death as described by Campbell and Muntzel are quite similar to the Mesmes situation. Their description of a single "once-fully-competent" speaker of Salvadoran Lenca is of particular interest here:

> We believe that his language may typify the radical language death situation, and we hypothesize general features based on it. For such a speaker, once fluent but not having made active use of his or her language in many years, recall is bound to be limited (see Elmendorf's [1981] "former speakers", Dorian's [1982b]

"formerly fluent") Typically the phonology is intact, with few if any deviations from the former native model, but much of the lexicon is forgotten or only recalled after strained pondering, more frequent and salient vocabulary items being retained better than others. The grammar, as well, may be largely the same as the native model in its fully viable state, although actual production is characterized by fairly simple constructions and phrases, with reduced access to stylistic or pragmatic variants and complex sentences: such speakers are unable (at least initially) to produce a normal discourse. Situations which give rise to such a speaker may or may not produce so-called semi-speakers; in the case of Salvadoran Lenca, which we have treated as potentially typical of radical death, there are none (Campbell and Muntzel 1989:183–184)

Both the lack of semi-speakers of Salvadoran Lenca and the maintenance of the grammatical system are quite similar to Mesmes. As has already been alluded to and is discussed below in greater detail in 3.5, the grammatical constructions found in the Mesmes text are representative of the other Gurage languages in the subgroup. However, while Abegaz did pause and reiterate while speaking Mesmes, he does not appear to have had any significant trouble in producing "normal discourse" as Campbell and Muntzel predict.

3.5 The "Later Loss" Hypothesis and "Rusty Speakers"

The Mesmes situation manifests some similarities with both the gradual death and radical death models. But neither can fully account for all the phenomena. It does appear, based on all the available information, that the shift from Mesmes to Hadiyya and the subsequent death of Mesmes happened quickly. Abegaz mentioned that he spoke Mesmes as a first language, but by the time he was married, probably in his early twenties, the language of the home domain was Hadiyya. According to his testimony, Abegaz's children never learned to speak Mesmes. Abegaz did, however, continue speaking Mesmes with his brother until about thirty years ago. That is, while normal transmission may have stopped some time around the 1940s or 1950s, Abegaz and his brother continued speaking Mesmes to each other until the early 1970s. So then, what sort of speaker or semi-speaker is Abegaz?

Sasse follows Menn (1989) in adding the category *rusty speaker* to the continuum of semi-speakers proposed in the literature (Sasse 1992b:62).

The rusty speaker, Sasse argues, is a speaker who has learned the language through what he calls "regular" acquisition but then has lost his/her competence through "the lack of regular linguistic experience" (Sasse 1992b:62). He writes:

> Those children who are socialized completely in the obsolescent language may forget it later due to the lack of communication partners; i.e. the regular continuation of language acquisition by intersubjective communication during adulthood does not occur. In other words, the continuum among semi-speakers and between semi-speakers and rusty speakers may be viewed as a continuum between random acquisition as the one extreme, and varying degrees of "regular" acquisition. (Sasse 1992b:63)

In the case of Mesmes, then, the terminal speaker is likely a rusty speaker who while not having had opportunity to speak Mesmes in the past thirty years, did learn the language through normal transmission and was thus fully competent, being able to continue use of the language in a severely limited communicative situation during adulthood. An examination of the Mesmes text is in order to determine if this rusty speaker's speech has undergone the sorts of changes indicative of other types of semi-speakers' language. This maintenance of Mesmes between brothers could certainly help account for how Abegaz's speech is atypical of radical death.

3.6 An Examination of the Mesmes Text in Light of the Linguistic Implications

The Mesmes text was recorded in Ast'ey K'ebele in May of 2001. The initial sentence-level free translation was provided by Abegaz himself, through a Hadiyya translator who conveyed the translation via Amharic.[4] I am indebted to Mr. Heyru Mohammed, an Ennemor Gurage speaker who lives in Dallas, Texas. He has helped me by providing a more detailed translation and offering some Ennemor examples for comparison where required.

The work of Hetzron, in *The Gunnän-Gurage Languages* (1977), provides the foundation upon which most of the following analysis is based. His interlinearization of Ennemor and Gyeto texts as well as his careful cross-dialectal analysis of Guragoid grammatical structures has provided me with the means for detailed parsing which would have otherwise been impossible. Another important source for comparative data is Leslau's

---

[4] The complete interlinearized transcription of the text is in appendix C.

3.6 An Examination of the Mesmes Text in Light of the Linguistic Implications

Etymological Dictionary of Gurage (1979), which provides lexical comparative data on all the major varieties of Gurage. Leslau's article, "The Verb Forms in Endegeny" (1992) has been essential in providing the morphological data linking Endegeny and Mesmes.

3.6.1 Possible examples of the impact of language death in the Mesmes text

As mentioned above, the morphological markings and grammatical structures found in the Mesmes text are very similar to those found in other Peripheral West Gurage languages. There are, however, a few unexpected phenomena which may be due, at least in part, to linguistic obsolescence.

First, the Amharic existential /nɛbbɛr/ is used eight times in the text (appendix C, lines 2–4, 10, and 11). There does not appear to be any particular reason for using the borrowed existential since the PWG form /banɛ-d/ is also used nearly as frequently (appendix C, lines 1, 6, 9, 12, and 13). This Amharic loan is not found in Hetzron's PWG text corpus (1977). The Kistane (Soddo) variety of Gurage does have the /nɛbbɛr/ form with the same durative-habitual meaning (Hetzron 1977:84). However, based on other evidence provided in chapter 4 concerning genetic subgrouping, it is unlikely that Mesmes would have inherited such a form. The most reasonable explanation is that the form is a borrowing from Amharic.

Of particular interest is the fact that Abegaz, the Mesmes speaker, is not a speaker of Amharic. While he was able to understand some simple questions in Amharic and probably possesses a degree of passive knowledge, he chose to speak Hadiyya to a Hadiyya-Amharic bilingual in order to communicate with me. His apparently inconsistent replacement of the existential with a borrowed form[5] may be the result either of language decay or of recall difficulties due to his status as a "rusty speaker."

Second, there appears to be a loss of contrast in marking between the 1S and 3SM prefixes for the imperfect[6] forms in Mesmes. This is most clearly evident in lines 1 and 2 in the text (from appendix C):

---

[5] Additional evidence that this form may indeed be borrowed is found in the lack of devoicing of the geminate second radical of the verb root; this devoicing is expected for all forms inherited via normal transmission (see also the comment on line 6 of the Mesmes text, in appendix D).

[6] In keeping with Hetzron 1977 and Leslau 1979, I am using the terms imperfect and perfect; these mostly closely correspond to Comrie's use of "imperfective" and "perfective" as the two basic aspectual distinctions in the language (Comrie 1976). The "perfect," as is used here, should not be understood to refer to a past event with present relevance, rather it is essentially an indication of the completeness of the event.

(1) aβo-ɲ   areʔ ɛ-wɔʔr   banɛ-d
    father-1SPO cow 3SM-guard.cattle   EXIST.PAST-MVM
    My father was watching cattle.

(2) aβo-ɲ   ti-kɛʃʃ-e   areʔ ɛ-wɔʔr   nɛbbɛr
    father.1SPO when-send-1SObj   cow 1S-guard.cattle   EXIST.PAST
    When my father sent me, I was watching cattle.

All PWG speakers who have translated these sentences have provided the same interpretation. It appears that the object-agreement marking in the subordinate verb /ti-kɛʃʃ-e/ and the contextual clues in line 2 are enough to identify the subject as 1S. While this phenomenon appears to be a reduction in marking of the agreement paradigm, it may be that this simplification is not due to any obsolescence process in Mesmes. Leslau, in his description of Endegeny verb forms, finds a similar neutralization, marking both 1S and 3S agreement prefixes in the imperfect as /i-/ (Leslau 1992:469). In a later endnote, Leslau questions his transcription,[7] "I may have recorded erroneously the singular, 1st person, with ə- instead of with ä-" (1992:473). In both Leslau and Hetzron's work it is quite clear that the other Gurage languages do not exhibit such neutralization between the 1st and 3rd singular imperfect prefixes (Leslau 1992, Hetzron 1977). Hetzron posits /ɛ-/ for 1S imperfect and /ji-/ for 3MS imperfect across the Gurage languages (1977:80). This is consistent with both the Ennemor and Gyeto texts (Hetzron 1977). Given this information, it appears that both Endegeny and Mesmes have lost contrast between the 1st and 3rd singular imperfect prefixes. Since Endegeny is still very much alive and is not likely to have undergone reductions indicative of language death processes, it seems best to treat this neutralization in the Mesmes text as an innovation, shared with Endegeny,[8] even though Endegeny and Mesmes have each chosen a different form for the basis of the leveling: Endegeny has leveled on the basis of the 3MS while Mesmes has leveled on the basis of the 1S.[9]

---

[7] In Leslau's transcription, the symbols ə and ä, correspond to the IPA i and ɛ, respectively.

[8] As will be shown in chapter 4, Endegeny and Mesmes do share a number of innovations, inviting the classification of a particular Endegeny/Mesmes subgroup (Hetzron 1977:79).

[9] There is also the possibility that Mesmes has simplified its prefixation for non-past verb forms. Where other Gurage languages maintain the distinction /ji-/ for the imperfect and /ɛ-/ for the jussive, it could be that Mesmes has extended the marker for jussive to mark the imperfect as well. For more discussion on the apparent leveling between 1S and 3S and the corresponding ∅- allomorphy before imperfect forms with initial /a/, see the note on line 6 in appendix D.

3.6 An Examination of the Mesmes Text in Light of the Linguistic Implications

There is also the possibility that some of the Mesmes pronominal paradigm has undergone leveling. In line 8, the form /hudua/ 'they' is the 3rd masculine plural pronoun. Leslau (1979) provides the 3M and 3MPL Endegeny forms as /hudɛ/ and /huno:/, respectively. An essential difference between the Endegeny singular and plural forms is the presence of the nasal in the latter. The same holds true for Ennemor, in which the forms for 3M and 3MPL are /xutɛ/ and /hunoa/ (Leslau 1979). It appears that Mesmes may have reanalyzed its pronominal paradigm, interpreting the final vowels of pronouns as agreement suffixes marking number. First, the Mesmes form /hudɛ/ or /hʊd/ serves as both the 3M pronoun as well as the definite marker. The same is true for Ennemor (Hetzron 1977:58). That is, this 3M pronoun/definite article occurs frequently and is thus a likely candidate to serve as a template for leveling. Second, the final vowel on the pronoun is /-ɛ/, which is homophonous with the 3M agreement suffix on the perfect forms of the verbs.[10] Also the final diphthong on the 3MPL pronoun, /-ua/, is identical to the 3MPL suffix on verbs in the perfect. Finally, it is possible that Mesmes speakers, or at the very least, this terminal speaker, has interpreted /hʊd/ to mean 3M and the final vowels /-ɛ/ and /-ua/ as denoting number, singular and plural, respectively.

In addition to these examples of leveling, there are a number of inconsistencies throughout the text that suggest, at the very least, the "rustiness" of the speaker. The PWG languages exhibit a suffix which is inherited from the Proto-Semitic main verb markers. The k/t/d[11] suffix is found on the main negative verbs, on relative nonpast forms, and on temporal forms in Gyeto, Ennemor, and Endegeny (Hetzron 1977:93). In the Mesmes text, however, the distribution of this suffix is less consistent.

ɛ-kɛʃʃ-ɛtʃtʃ-e-**dɨ**
REL-sent-3SF-1SOBJ-**SFX**

In this verb from line 4, the suffix, having undergone the alternation /t → d/, appears on the relative past form—an unexpected environment, given the distribution in other Peripheral West lects. In line 12, we find the suffix present on the temporal form, as expected. Yet, the same reflex is absent in the temporal constructions in lines 2, 11, and in each of the three examples in line 16. This inconsistency is not observed in Hetzron's Ennemor texts, where the behavior of the k/t/d suffix is far more regular.

---

[10] This final vowel is not present in the text; presumably, the Hadiyya practice of dropping final vowels in connected speech, while allowing them to surface in isolation, has spread to Mesmes.

[11] See appendix D, note on line 4 for a description of the allophonic distribution.

There is also an unexpected occurrence of the suffix on the perfect verb 'to give birth' in line 20.

Another inconsistency in the Mesmes text is the shape of the bound copula. The bound copula's recurring partial, that is the bound root of the copula construction, is the nasal /-n-/ (Hetzron 1977:106). Hetzron says that the shape of this copula in Ennemor is indicative of PWG lects in general.[12] The copula is bound, as the second-to-the-last element in the word, in PWG. Both the syntactic position and the shape of the copula are maintained in Mesmes, just as expected, in line 17:

geb : iri-nn-itɛ
farming-be.3M-SFX

Yet, in line 12, the shape of the copula is /-m-/:

ha : -ʔami-soj ʔ
that-be-time

This sort of allomorphy is not found elsewhere in PWG. There is nothing in the particular environments in these words to account for this inconsistency.

While the Mesmes text does contain these sorts of inconsistencies, as well as unexpected loanwords and a few possible examples of paradigmatic leveling, there is not much evidence to suggest that the language has undergone decay or reduction. In fact, each of these phenomena could be ascribed to the fact that the speaker himself is "rusty," not having spoken the language for approximately thirty years—though admittedly I make no attempt here to define what the speech of a rusty speaker would be like (see Menn 1989:345 for possibilities).

3.6.2 Evidence of maintenance of inherited structure in Mesmes

One of the most notable features in Gurage languages and Ethio-Semitic languages in general is extensive clausal conjoining. Hetzron comments:

> In Ethiopian languages temporal expressions are very important. The general tendency is to use long compound sentences instead of a sequence of simple ones. One way of compounding sentences is using converbial conjoining...but temporal constructions also play an important role (1977:99).

The converbial construction in Ethiopian languages is a chaining mechanism where a series of verbs or entire clauses is linked together with

---

[12] For a more complete analysis of this copula, see the note on line 8 in appendix D.

3.6 An Examination of the Mesmes Text in Light of the Linguistic Implications 39

only the final verb carrying tense/aspect marking for the entire complex. Each of the conjoined verbs carries marking particular to verbs in converbial constructions as well as communicating person and number through the same marking found on other verb forms. All the Gurage languages exhibit the so-called m-converb (Hetzron 1977:94). In the PWG languages, the m-converb marker takes the form /-m$^{(w)}$/ in the 2FSG, 2MPL, and 3MPL (Hetzron 1977:84). In the other persons, the PWG m-converb marking is the same as that found in the Gura variety: the final vowel of the verb is stressed and where no final vowel is present, the epenthetic [ɨ] is added finally to carry the stress (Hetzron 1977:84).[13] While Hetzron does not offer any statement regarding whether the PWG and Gura alternating forms or the non-alternating /-m/ found elsewhere in Gurage is the innovation, it could be reasonably assumed, given Hetzron's subgrouping for Outer South Ethiopic (figure 1.2), that PWG should exhibit an innovation. A single innovation found throughout the rest of Gurage would be much less expected. This being the case, it is then likely that the stressing of the final vowel in the Gura and PWG varieties is due to a compensatory-like process where the loss of the final /-m/ marker leads to a stressed vowel (probably long in duration/timing).[14] Hetzron notes this exact process with the loss of the main past ending /-m/ in some Gurage languages:

> If the basic stress rule is applied to the Chaha past tense forms, we obtain säpär'äm/säpär'ä. This -m has completely disappeared in Gura, it disappeared after short vowels in PWG (also after the feminine plural in Gyeto). The drop of the -m, however, did not lead to a readjustment of the stress in accordance with the basic stress rule. The earlier, positionally no more justified, stress was maintained as an allomorphic exponent of *-m, i.e. säpär'ä/säp'ärä for main/subordinate (1977:42–43).

Thus, despite the loss of the coda on the formerly closed syllable, the stress of that syllable was maintained, marking the verb's status as the main past. This main past ending /-m/[15] is not to be confused with the

---

[13] The stress here is certainly marked in that normal stress in PWG (Ennemor, specifically) is penultimate when the final syllable is open (Hetzron 1977:42). It is crucial to note that these converbs all end in open syllables, yet receive ultimate stress.

[14] There is another possibility as well: that PWG and Gura retain the original heterogeneity and that the other languages regularized the converb system by generalizing the /-m/ to cover all persons. Thus, the other languages would have undergone analogical leveling. This would imply, however, an upside-down view of the historical tree for Outer South Ethiopic.

[15] Hetzron appears to suggest that the /-m/ main past ending (which is identical to the m-converb in the perfect form) is related to the /-m/ enclitic—a highly multifunctional element which can mark coordination between nouns, can establish links between related

m-converb ending. Hetzron, in his parsing of the Ennemor texts, glosses the stressing of the final vowel which marks the converbial construction in PWG as *C* (see line 6 of Ennemor text 19 in Hetzron 1977:236), and he marks the stressing of the final vowel which marks main past marker and the related /-m/ enclitic as *M*. That is, while the form is identical between these two markers today, their functions point to their separate origins.[16]

What is most central to this converbial conjoining discussion is that this type of marked embedding is found throughout the Mesmes text (lines: 6, 7, 10, 12, 13, 14, 15, 17, and 18). As mentioned earlier, Maher says coordination is preferred to embedding (1991). The nature of the converb, as a verb which is morphologically marked as part of a serial string and not as a main verb, is more like embedding than simple coordination, even though converbs may also be used to indicate the latter. The complex syntactic relationships communicated via converbial constructions are not indicative of the sorts of syntactic simplification found in many dying languages.[17]

Another internal change indicative of language death is the decay of verbal morphology. This is not present in Mesmes. Many of the verbal markers found in Hetzron's Ennemor texts can be readily identified in Mesmes: the causative /a-/ (line: 7), the temporal /t-/ (lines: 2, 5, 12, 14, and 16), the relative perfect prefix /ɛ-/ (lines: 4, 10, 12, and 16), the negative[18] (relative) prefix /aɲ-/ (lines: 10 and 11), the passive[19] /t-/ (lines: 4 and 16), the purposive /-i/ (lines: 10, 12, and 17) and the all the various subject and object agreement morphology found throughout the text.

---

topics and can also make reference to topics already established in earlier discourse (Hetzron 1977:129). Perhaps the clearest example that these two forms are related is found in Hetzron's use of the single M as a grammatical reference marker for the main past marker as well as for the enclitic (1977:143). For more on the main past marker, see the note on line 4 in appendix D.

[16] Perhaps a more serious challenge in the analysis of these Gurage languages is the nature of the converb itself. If the converb marking (on subordinate verbs) is identical to the main past marking (on main verbs), what is implied about the nature of converbs in these languages? In texts where the most frequently used tense is past and the subjects of the converbials is 3S, there would be a loss of contrast between the main and the subordinate verbs—all would be marked with the same ending, the stressed final vowel.

[17] There is the possibility that the converbial construction is maintained because of its prevalence in the language area and its existence in Hadiyya (see Hudson's "Conjunctive" 1976:269).

[18] In the other Gurage languages (apart from Mesmes), the negative prefix is listed as /an-/ as opposed to one ending in a palatal nasal found in Mesmes (Hetzron 1977:87, Leslau 1992:468).

[19] See the note on line 4 in appendix D for a discussion of the impact of the passive on the first radical of the verb root in the imperfect form.

3.6 An Examination of the Mesmes Text in Light of the Linguistic Implications 41

In short, based on the large number of morphological, syntactic, and lexical reflexes found in the Mesmes text which correspond directly to other Peripheral West Gurage lects, the text appears to be a reliable source for Mesmes data. There is very little evidence of loss of syntactic structure or simplification of morphological paradigms in the data, and the few inconsistencies and possible levelings could be attributed to the "rusty" status of the speaker.

4

The Genetic Position of Mesmes

4.1 The Establishment of Mesmes as a Gurage Language

As noted in 1.6.2, Hetzron, upon examination of Bender and Stinson's wordlist and grammatical information, claimed that Mesmes was closely related to Endegeny. This claim, however, was not explicitly substantiated by data and analysis. In fact, the grammatical paradigms that Bender and Stinson collected were never published. In order to evaluate the comparative evidence for linking Mesmes with Gurage and then with Peripheral West Gurage in particular, an examination of Bender and Stinson's wordlist and grammatical paradigms and my own Mesmes text is in order. These three sources of linguistic data comprise the entire Mesmes corpus.

I am assuming that the details discussed in the upcoming sections are likely some of the phenomena that Hetzron observed, leading him to posit a close relationship between Mesmes and Endegeny.

4.1.1 The ethnonym as evidence of Guragoid placement

As mentioned in section 2.3.3, the Mesmes ethnonym /mɨsmɨs/ is a reduplication of the Gurage reflex /mɨs/ 'man' to express the meaning 'people'. According to Leslau (1979), /mɨs/ is still retained in the Muher and Kistane varieties. Based on wordlists that I gathered, the term has also been found in Gyeto and Ezha and in the Desa variety of Muher. While this link with the Gurage languages cannot be argued to be conclusive evidence of genetic relationship, it would be unlikely for one group (the Gurage) to assign a name like *Mesmes* 'the people' to a group other than themselves. When coupled with the comparative evidence below, a more complete picture emerges, linking the Mesmes and recognized Gurage languages in history.

4.1.2 The main verb marker retention attesting to a genetic link with Gurage

While true comparative work utilizing the comparative method would not permit the use of retentions as evidence of any specific shared history between a set of languages, retentions may still be useful to the linguist involved in historical research. Retentions, assuming they are not borrowed features and they do not rely on the so-called *Wanderwörter* (examples of shared vocabulary in a linguistic area among unrelated or non-closely related languages), do in fact attest to a common genetic origin. They cannot, however, be used to establish degrees of relatedness such as subgroups within a larger family (see, e.g., Campbell 2004).

In the Mesmes text (appendix C), lines 1 and 13 show an important and rare retention found only among select Guragoid languages. In each of these lines is found /banɛd/, the past form of the existential verb /banɛ/, marked with zero for third person masculine and with the final /-d/ to indicate the main verb. These main verb markers, found in Outer South Ethiopic, can be traced to Proto-Semitic elements (Hetzron 1972:37). Their presence in the Mesmes text on only the past existentials is indicative of the relationship between Mesmes and the Peripheral West Gurage languages:

> Western Gurage dropped these markers altogether. They have survived only in the Past tense form of the verb "there is" in Peripheral West Gurage: Enär Sg. 3m. baanä-dä, f. baanäčə-dä, Pl. 3m. baanäwa-tä, 3f. baanaa-tä, where -dä represents -t, the suffix used after Complements of Sg. 3m./f. and -tä corresponds to -tt attested in Muxər [Muher] (Hetzron 1972:38)

While this evidence does not prove a particular subgrouping within Peripheral West Gurage, it does suggest that the Mesmes language is historically related to Gurage, and to PWG in particular, although the possibility of borrowing cannot be entirely ruled out.

4.1 The Establishment of Mesmes as a Gurage Language

4.1.3 Morpho-syntactic evidence of Guragoid relationship

The Mesmes text also provides a good deal of morphological and syntactic evidence of relationship between Mesmes and the other Gurage languages. This is described briefly in section 3.6.2.[1] It is known that borrowing may indeed include lexical features as well as morpho-grammatical and even syntactic features (Thomason and Kaufman 1988, Seliger and Vago 1991). Yet, it must be assumed that shared phonological innovations attested in entire systems (a language's verbal morphology) would be more persuasive evidence than phonological shared innovations in unrelated lexical items. Thomason and Kaufman argue that a language must show linguistic evidence of relationship with its ancestors in both lexical and grammatical subsystems before it can be classified as a so-called "genetic language" (1988).

Table 4.1 offers evidence of relationship between Mesmes and other Ethiopian-Semitic and, specifically, Peripheral West Gurage (PWG) lects through an examination of PWG verbal morphology as found in Hetzron 1977 and Mesmes verbal morphology as found in the Mesmes text. Essentially, all the morphology in table 4.1 is identical, excluding the negative prefix, the nasal of which is palatalized in Mesmes.[2] Even the allomorphy involving the passive-reflexive prefix is the same in Mesmes as in other Gurage (and Ethio-Semitic) languages in general. The causative, temporal, negative, and passive-reflexive markers are found widely throughout Ethiopian-Semitic while the phonologically reduced relative-marker (of a genitive source) and the purposive are unique to PWG (Leslau 1979; Hetzron 1977:99).

---

[1] For more detailed analysis of the sorts of morphological and syntactic evidence the Mesmes text offers, see appendix D.

[2] This palatalization on the negative prefix may be due to an underlying initial /j/ on the relative prefix. This /j/ is not found in relatives without the negative, but there is a possibly related phenomenon where the epenthetic vowel is raised to /i/—again possibly a reflex of a historical /j/. See note 11 in appendix D.

Table 4.1. Mesmes and PWG Verbal Morphology Comparison

Verbal Morphology	PWG form	Mesmes form	Location in Mesmes Text
Causative	a-	a-	7
Temporal	t-	t-	2,5,12,14,16
Negative*	an-	aɲ-	10,12
Passive-Reflexive**	t- / C:	t- / C:	4,16
Relative Marker for Perfect	ɛ-	ɛ-	4,10,12,16
Purposive	-i	-i	19,11,17

* The negative prefix is only found in the Mesmes text on relative clauses, though it is expected to be the general form for the negative.

** See the note on line 4 in appendix D for a discussion of the allomorphy involving the passive/reflexive prefix in the environment of other prefixes in the imperfect.

The word order of Gurage languages is summed up by Hetzron: Time-adverb – Subject – Complement(s) – Verb (1977:114). In the Mesmes text, the first half of line 1 provides an example of this ordering:[3]

    iʃi   bɛ-tɛʔeɲɲawʊd   aβo-ɲ   areʔɛ-wɔʔr
    okay at-birth/childhood father-1SPO cow3SM-guard.cattle
    banɛ-d
    EXIST.PAST-MVM
    Okay, during (my) childhood, my father was taking care of cattle.

The SOV order with time adverbials in front is preserved completely here. As in other Gurage languages, the relative clauses (and all modifiers, for that matter) precede the modified element (Hetzron 1977:115). This is clear in lines 4 and 10: /aβo-ɲ ɛ-keʃʃ-u wɛd/ 'father-1SPO REL.-sent-3MP place' and /aɲ-ɛ-ʔeɲɲɛ hʊd/ 'NEG-REL-give.birth he.'

---

[3] It may be argued, however, that the initial sentence of a discourse may be a pragmatically marked utterance and not a good example of canonical order. This word order finds partial support in line 7, where all elements are present save the 1S pronoun, which is not required in Ethio-Semitic languages unless emphasis is needed. This pronoun's position in Mesmes would be after the initial adverbial.

4.1.4 Lexical evidence of close relationship with PWG

There is also lexical evidence that Mesmes is closely related to the Peripheral West Gurage lects. Table 4.2 provides a summary of the words in the Mesmes corpus (wordlist and text) that appear to be unique to the Peripheral West languages according to Leslau's *Etymological Dictionary of Gurage* (1979). That is, these words are not found in other Gurage languages and are found in at least some of the Peripheral West speech forms.[4]

Table 4.2. Lexemes Unique to Mesmes and PWG

Gloss	Mesmes word	Source for Mesmes	Endegeny	Ennemor	Gyeto	Source for PWG
to send	kɛʃʃɛ	text 2,4	kɛʃʃɛ	kɛʃʃɛ	x	Leslau 1979
children	de:ŋga	text 2,7,8,20	x	de:ŋgʲa	x	Hetzron 1977:244
now	waʔaka	text 8,16,17	waʔakkɛ	waʔaka	x	Leslau 1979
to give	i:m	text 9	x	jɨ:m	x	Hetzron 1977:238
to beg	saʔarɛ	text 10,11	saʔarɛ	saʔarɛ	saʔarɛ	Leslau 1979
to spend the night	ɲɛʔɛ	text 18	ɲɛʔɛ	neʔɛ	x	Leslau 1979
good	mo'ʔo	wordlist 33	muʔ	moʔ	x	Leslau 1979
mountain / hill	a:nja	wordlist 53	aɲɲɛ	ʔaɲɛ	aɲɛ	Leslau 1979
road	mo:ja	wordlist 65	mejɛ	meja	mɛja	Leslau 1979
to stand	-tɛʃɛkkɔ-	wordlist 77	(tɛ)ʃɛkkɛ:	(tɛ)ʃɛkɛβɛ	(tɛ)ʃɛkɛβɛ	Leslau 1979
this	wʊ:	wordlist 84	wɑ	wɑ:	x	Leslau 1979
wet (adj.)	ir'ramo	wordlist 94	i:rɛ	x	x	Leslau 1979

Due to Hetzron's texts, there is substantially more data available on Ennemor than Endegeny, and it is my opinion that the lexical forms for 'children' and 'to give' that are provided in Ennemor but not in Endegeny

---

[4] Of course, it may simply be the case that some of these forms do in fact exist in non-PWG lects but that they have not yet been documented as such in the literature.

may actually exist in Endegeny.⁵ The best set of Endegeny data is that which is found in Leslau's dictionary. It must be noted that Leslau did not find these two forms (for 'children' and 'to give') in Ennemor either. There are also five words in the Mesmes text which have not been found in any other Gurage language. It is unknown if some of these are borrowings or uniquely Mesmes terms: /jɛsizi : ʔ/ (lines 5 and 6), /anɨkk/ (line 6), /sojgiʔ/ (lines 9 and 12), /tuiʔioi/ (line 14), /wɛdkɛ/ (line 20).⁶ In the Mesmes wordlist (appendix A with notes and appendix B with the Hadiyya and Kambaata comparison), there are four additional words which appear to be unique to Mesmes: /k'ɔk'ɔ/ (5) 'big', /nu : ba/ (39) 'heart', /k'ok'o/⁷ (50) 'many', /t'o : na/ (67) 'sand'.

In short, the Mesmes autoethnonym, the retention of the main verb markers, the nearly identical verbal morphology and syntax, as well as the lexicon all suggest that Mesmes is closely related to other Gurage languages, PWG in particular. This is enough evidence to establish the "assumed relatedness" that Campbell (2000) considers an essential precursor to using the comparative method in determining historical subgroupings.

4.2 Shared Innovations Linking Mesmes with PWG

As mentioned in 4.1.2, in keeping with the time-tested comparative method, only shared linguistic innovations can be considered as conclusive evidence of closely shared history. Retentions may point to some genetic relationship (though they offer no subgrouping insight), but they may also be present due to borrowings.

If, for instance, lects A, B, C, and D are related genetically and C and D both attest to a number of identical changes that are not in A or in B, one may assume that C and D have shared some history. That is, C and D are closely related, having at one time been one lect. This is, of course, a simplification of the historical process, but will suffice for now.⁸

---

⁵ The etymon represented by the Mesmes /i : m/ 'to give' appears to be cognate with the same verb in Proto-Omotic (Bender, personal communication, 2004).

⁶ For possible glosses for some of these terms, see the corresponding line notes in appendix D.

⁷ This word 'many' is likely related to (if not the same as) the word 'big' (5).

⁸ For a more complete discussion of the comparative method, its methodologies and historical sound change in general, see Campbell 2000.

4.2 Shared Innovations Linking Mesmes with PWG

4.2.1 Innovations in the pronominal paradigm

In table 4.3 are found the pronominal paradigms for Mesmes, Endegeny, Ennemor, Gyeto, and Cheha. Of all the speech varieties in the chart, only Cheha is a non-Peripheral West Gurage lect, according to Hetzron's classification. Its inclusion here is to provide for comparison a representative Central West Gurage (CWG) form that did not participate in the PWG innovations.

In the following tables, unless otherwise specified, the Mesmes pronominal data are from Bender and Stinson's unpublished fieldnotes; the other Mesmes data are from Bender's wordlist (1971). The other Gurage data are taken from Leslau's *Etymological Dictionary of Gurage* (1979). In table 4.3, all the data have been "regularized" by converting the phonetic representations to the more standard International Phonetic Alphabet.

Table 4.3. Mesmes, PWG, and Cheha Pronominal Paradigms

Gloss	Mesmes	Endegeny	Ennemor	Gyeto	Cheha
1 S	hijja	ijɛ	ɨja	ɨja	ɨja
1 PL	inna	inɛ	ina	ina	jina
2 M S	ahe	ahɛ	axɛ	axɛ	axɛ
2 M PL	ahu : we	ahu	axɨwa	axɨβa / axwa / axuwa	axu
2 F S	a : ʃe	aʃɛ	aʃa	axʲa	axʲa / axʲ
2 F PL	ahu : we	aha :	axa :	axma	axma
3 M S	hʊde	hudɛ	xuda	xuta	xut(a)
3 M PL	hahunje	huno :	xɨnowa	xɨnowa / xɨnɛwa	xɨno
3 F S	ʃi : di	ʃidɛ	xʲida	xʲita	xʲita
3 F PL	hahunje	hina	xɨna :	xɨnɛma	xɨnɛma

The most prevalent innovation in terms of sound correspondences in the data above is /x:h/. Consistently, where Cheha, Gyeto, and Ennemor have the velar fricative /x/, both Mesmes and Endegeny have the /h/. Table 4.4 isolates only those lexemes where the correspondence is evident.

Table 4.4. The Sound Correspondence /x:h/ in the Pronominal Paradigms

Gloss	Mesmes	Endegeny	Ennemor	Gyeto	Cheha
2 M S	ahe	ahɛ	axɛ	axɛ	axɛ
2 M PL	ahu : we	ahu	axɨwa	axɨβa / axwa / axuwa	axu
2 F PL	ahu : we	aha :	axa :	axma	axma
3 M S	hʊde	hudɛ	xuda	xuta	xut(a)
3 M PL	hahunje	huno :	xɨnowa	xɨnowa / xɨnɛwa	xɨno
3 F PL	hahunje	hɨna	xɨna :	xɨnɛma	xɨnɛma

It is important to consider the directionality here. There are two possibilities. Either the more widespread /x/ became /h/ in Mesmes and Endegeny or the /h/ is the older form and became /x/ everywhere else, being retained as /h/ only in Mesmes and Endegeny. Phonologically speaking, the /x/ is more marked than the /h/, being less common in the phonological inventories of the world's languages, acquired later by mature speakers and more subject to change across time (Faingold 1996). That is, it would be expected, given the general trend of markedness reduction, that the /x/ would weaken to the /h/. Thus, /x/ → /h/ in Endegeny and Mesmes is the most plausible direction, given that there is no evidence to suggest that the reverse order is more likely.

In table 4.5, the palatalized voiceless velar fricative /xʲ/ becomes the voiceless palatal fricative /ʃ/ in Endegeny and Mesmes, and sometimes in Ennemor.

Table 4.5. The Sound Correspondence /xʲ:ʃ/ in the Pronominal Paradigms

Gloss	Mesmes	Endegeny	Ennemor	Gyeto	Cheha
2 F S	a : ʃe	aʃɛ	aʃa	axʲa	axʲa / axʲ
3 F S	ʃi : di	ʃidɛ	xʲida	xʲita	xʲita

The example of 3rd feminine singular in Ennemor does not show the change; it is not known why it does not. In the bound forms (discussed in chapter 5), I show that Ennemor does participate in the innovation consistently. The form in table 4.5 appears to be an anomaly. There is no distributional constraint in Ennemor, limiting the /ʃ/ to non-initial environments.

4.2 Shared Innovations Linking Mesmes with PWG

The final sound change in these pronominal data involves the correspondence /t:d/:

Table 4.6. The Sound Correspondence /t:d/ in the Pronominal Paradigms

Gloss	Mesmes	Endegeny	Ennemor	Gyeto	Cheha
3 M S	hʊde	hʊdɛ	xuda	xuta	xut(a)
3 F S	ʃi : di	ʃidɛ	xʲida	xʲita	xʲita

The data in table 4.6 show the sound correspondence /t:d/, where Gyeto and Cheha have /t/ and Mesmes, Endegeny, and Ennemor have /d/. The pronominal paradigm exhibits this phenomenon in the intervocalic position only, which would be rather easily explained as voicing due to the environment. However, this /t:d/ correspondence does appear across the board—initially, medially, and finally.

Table 4.7. The Sound Correspondence /t:d/ in 'house'

Gloss	Lexemes	Speech variety*
house	bet	Gura
	ge	Kistane
	bet	Mesqan
	bet	Muher
	bet	Cheha
	bet	Ezha
	bet	Desa
	be : t	Gyeto
	bi : d	Ennemor
	bi : d	Endegeny
	bi : de	Mesmes

*The data on Gura and Desa are from unpublished wordlists gathered as a part of the Gurage language survey by Ahland and Ahland (2001). In terms of intelligibility, Gura is part of Sebat Bet, and Desa is a sub-dialect of Muher. An interesting isogloss which distinguishes Desa from Muher is the use of the Kistane/Soddo 1S pronoun /ɛdi/ in Desa as opposed to the /anɛ/ found elsewhere in Muher. Hetzron (1977:5) considered Desa to be a variety of Soddo (Kistane), but the Gurage language survey research and interviews with the speakers in the area has shown Desa to be a variety of Muher.

Here, again, is found the /t:d/ correspondence. This time, however, the change occurs word-finally (though it has become non-final in Mesmes).

Tables 4.7 and 4.8 provide evidence of the additional innovation of relevant vocalic length. Hetzron (1977) deals with this phenomenon in Peripheral West Gurage, though its occurrence in Mesmes is not discussed. This vocalic length is indeed contrastive. In Ennemor, Hetzron found that the long vowels behave phonologically as a sequence of vowels, evidenced by stress patterns such as /bi`id/ (1977:36). Unfortunately, the Mesmes data are not consistently marked for stress. Essentially, everywhere long vowels are found in Gyeto, Ennemor, and Endegeny, they are found in Mesmes—excellent evidence for their shared history.[9]

Table 4.8. The Sound Correspondence /t:d/ in 'fire'

Gloss	Lexemes	Speech variety
fire (n)	isɑt	Gura
	ɛsɑt	Kistane
	isɑt	Mesqan
	isɑt	Muher
	isɑt	Cheha
	isɑt	Ezha
	isɑt	Desa
	isɑ : t / isɑ : t	Gyeto
	isɑ : d	Ennemor
	isɑ : d	Endegeny
	isɑ : de	Mesmes

It must be pointed out, however, that just as the intervocalic environment in table 4.6 is not responsible for the voicing of the /t/, neither is the long vowel/geminate vowel sequence responsible for its voicing in tables 4.7 or 4.8. In table 4.9, the /t/ to /d/ voicing is in an environment lacking a long vowel.

---

[9] Section 4.2.4.2. discusses the innovation of vocalic length in more detail.

4.2 Shared Innovations Linking Mesmes with PWG

Table 4.9. The Sound Correspondence /t:d/ in 'neck'

Gloss	Lexemes	Speech variety
neck	angɛt	Gura
	angɛt	Kistane
	angɛt	Mesqan
	angɛt	Muher
	angɛt	Cheha
	angɛt	Ezha
	angɛt	Desa
	angɛt	Gyeto
	angɛd	Ennemor
	angɛd	Endegeny
	angɔda	Mesmes

The voicing of the /t/ to /d/ in the initial environment is discussed in 4.2.3 as part of the examination of relative chronology. Considering that the /t/ is voiced in all environments in Ennemor, Endegeny, and Mesmes, it must be noted that this is a reversal of the expected trend in markedness reduction. There is, however, higher order motivation for this reversal of markedness reduction.

4.2.2 Markedness reversal and the beginnings of an obstruent chain shift

It appears that the PWG subgroup underwent at least the beginnings of a chain shift. The data are inconsistent, most likely attesting to the fact that the shift was never completed. Nonetheless, there are quite a few examples where the Outer South Ethiopic proto obstruent, when it is geminate, is devoiced in Gyeto, Ennemor, and Endegeny (table 4.10). Devoicing of geminate obstruents is by no means a surprise, given that it is more difficult articulatorily to maintain voicing as the length of stop closure increases. Unfortunately, due to the limited size of the Mesmes wordlist, no examples of such devoicing are found. The lexemes where this occurs are not in the wordlist.

Table 4.10. The Sound Correspondence /dd:t/ in 'to throw down'

Gloss	Lexemes	Speech variety
to throw down	addɛgɛ	Kistane
	addɛgɛ	Mesqan
	addɛgɛ	Muher
	ad ɛgɛ	Cheha
	addɛgɛ	Ezha
	at ɛgɛ	Gyeto
	at ɛgɛ	Ennemor
	attɛgɛ	Endegeny

There are, however, two examples of this same devoicing phenomenon in the Mesmes text. In line 7, the verb for 'to marry' shows the same pattern in Mesmes (appendix C):

bɛ-ha : da   wa : da de : ɲga-ɲo   gɛ : ɾɛd   **a-gɛʔpa-ˈhu**
after-that   that   children-1SPO   girl   CAUSE-marry-1S.CONV

Elsewhere in Gurage, the word is as follows: Cheha /(a)gɛpa-m/, Ezha /(a)gɛbba-m/, Ennemor /(a)gɛpa/, Endegeny /(a)gɛppaʔa/, and Gyeto /(a)gɛpa/. Just as in table 4.10, the form in Ezha is voiced and geminate, while the corresponding form in PWG is voiceless, with gemination maintained only in Endegeny. The other example is ti-n-t-akkɨd in line 16; see discussion in appendix D of this example of /gg/ → /kk/.

Before going on, it must be noted that only some Gurage lects have maintained geminate consonants: Kistane, Mesqan, Muher, Ezha, and Endegeny. The innovation is the loss of the distinction between geminate and non-geminate consonants and does not appear to correspond to any particular shared history.[10] In any case, the devoicing under discussion occurs with other lengthened obstruents as well:

---

[10] That is to say, the loss of long consonants (geminate sequences, phonologically), does not cluster with other innovations. Rather, these lects appear to have undergone this markedness reduction apart from one another.

4.2 Shared Innovations Linking Mesmes with PWG

Table 4.11. The Sound Correspondence /bb:p/ in 'to skin'

Gloss	Lexemes	Speech variety
to skin	t'ɛbbɑ	Kistane
	t'ɛbbɑ	Mesqan
	t'ɛbbɑ	Muher
	t'ɛp ɑ	Cheha
	t'ɛbbɑ	Ezha
	t'ɛp ɑ	Gyeto
	ʔɛp ɑ	Ennemor
	ʔɛppɑ	Endegeny

In table 4.11, the /bb/ is devoiced in Peripheral West. The change also occurs in Cheha. It is likely that this beginning of a chain shift could provide the so-called higher order motivation which helps to account for the /t/ → /d/ voicing in Peripheral West, i.e., sound chain shifts appeal to restructurings of the larger phonological system and are not restricted to individual sounds and their individual values on a markedness scale.

4.2.3 An examination of the systematicity of relative chronology in the Mesmes data

Because of the large corpus of Gurage data in Leslau's dictionary (1979), and because of Hetzron's comparative work,[11] it is possible to trace the relative chronology of some sound changes by beginning with my proposed Outer South Ethiopic proto-form and observing the changes leading up to the Mesmes form found in Bender's data. I have not yet attempted an entire consistent reconstruction of Outer South Ethiopic, but have only worked through the proto-forms for the 99-item Mesmes wordlist, for the purpose of showing the proposed relative ordering of these sound changes in the data.[12]

---

[11] Because the Mesmes corpus is so limited, Hetzron's comparative work in the rest of Gurage is particularly important. I rely on some of his well-documented innovations in Gurage to help to identify the same changes in Mesmes.

[12] While using Leslau's dictionary as a great resource, I do not rely on his proto forms. As noted earlier, Leslau holds that there is a single parent for all Gurage (including Silt'e, Wolane, Zway, etc.). I have relied on Hetzron's trees and thus only wish to posit reconstructions which will account for the daughters of Outer South Ethiopic.

Table 4.12. Guragoid and Mesmes Forms for 'leaf'

Gloss	Lexemes	Speech variety
leaf	k ' ɨt ' e	Muher
	k ' ɨt ' e	Desa
	k ' ɨt ' ɛl	Kistane
	k ' ɨt ' ɛl	Mesqan
	k ' ɨt ' ɛr	Gura
	k ' ɨt ' ɛr	Ezha
	k ' ɨt ' ɛɾ	Cheha
	k ' ɨt ' ɛɾ	Gyeto
	k ɛʔ ɛɾ	Ennemor
	k ɛʔ ɛɾ	Endegeny
	k oʔ oɾa	Mesmes

Table 4.12 provides the various forms of the lexeme 'leaf' in the same Gurage varieties which have been considered above. The data provide a look at the reflexes found in the daughters of Outer South Ethiopic today. The changes from the proposed proto-form may now be traced down to the current form in Mesmes.

To begin with, I posit the form /*k ' ɨt ' ɛl/ as the proto-form. Table 4.13 traces the various changes as they apply, working up to the realization in Mesmes. By examining which changes occur in which varieties, it is possible to begin to reconstruct the relative ordering or time-depth of the sound changes in the data.[13]

---

[13] The rules (1a) and (1b) in tables 4.13 and 4.15, respectively, occur at the same relative time-depth. This is apparent since the languages exhibiting this change are the same. The rules (3a) and (3b) in table 4.15 are also numbered in like manner to show that they too occur at the same relative time-depth, affecting Endegeny, Ennemor, and Mesmes.

4.2 Shared Innovations Linking Mesmes with PWG

Table 4.13. The Relative Chronology as Evidenced in 'leaf'

Rules	*k'ɨt'ɛl
1a.	*l > r
	k'ɨt'ɛr
2.	*k' > k
	kɨt'ɛr
3a.	*t' > ʔ
	kɨʔɛr
4.	vowel changes
	/koʔorɑ/

First is found the rule *l > r. This is a sound change which occurs as part of a larger series of changes involving the liquids, l/n/r (Hetzron 1977). For the argument here, it is enough to note that proto /*l/ becomes /r/ word-finally, as follows:

1a. *l > r in Gura, Ezha, Cheha, Gyeto, Ennemor, Endegeny, Mesmes (Hetzron's CPWG group)
   > ∅ in Muher, Desa

That is, essentially this change occurs in the same lects that inherited the innovation of the two future tenses (CPWG group). This change (1a) is the first change to occur to the proto-form; that is, it occurs at a time-depth earlier than the other changes. This is made obvious by the vast number of lects where the change is consistently found. The loss of the word-final /r/ in Muher and Desa appears to be a later innovation in those two lects.

The next sound change (rule 2 in table 4.13) to occur in history affects only Endegeny, Ennemor, and Mesmes. That is, it must have occurred at a time after Gyeto had separated from the other Peripheral West varieties. This *deglottalization* rule can be generalized as follows:

2. *C' > C /#___V(C)(V)C' 'deglottalization'   in Ennemor, Endegeny, Mesmes

Basically, there is a dissimilatory process here where the first of two glottalized consonants occurring in a phonological word is deglottalized. The second is left intact. This process only occurs when two ejective (glottalized) consonants are found in the same word.

The following rule also affects Ennemor, Endegeny, and Mesmes. Rule 3a is a *debuccalization* process where the place features of the glottalized consonant (ejective) are lost and only the glottal remains. While Hetzron does not generalize this rule with any formalism, he does make mention of the process (1977). This debuccalization[14] merger took place at a slightly more recent time-depth than rule 2 and occurs in every environment:

3a. *C' > ʔ   'debuccalization'   in Ennemor, Endegeny, Mesmes

Finally, after this rule applies, a series of vowel changes take place in the Mesmes form. Vowel length is discussed in 4.2.4.2, while other vocalic phenomena are discussed in section 4.2.4.3. It is assumed that some of these vocalic changes, such as the final vocalism, are due to contact with Hadiyya (discussed in chapter 5). The stem vowels have undergone a backing process and a final vowel has been added. The deglottalization and debuccalization find additional support when one considers data from other South Ethiopic languages, such as Amharic. The ejectives seen in tables 4.13 and 4.15 are clearly attested outside Outer South Ethiopic as well.

The regularity of these changes (not including the vocalic phenomena evident only in Mesmes) is clearly seen in that they apply to sets of lects which have already been seen to subgroup together on the basis of other innovations.

One more example of relative chronology will be considered before other processes are examined: The proposed Outer South Ethiopic proto-form for 'moon' or 'moonlight' is /*t'ɛr:ak'a/.

---

[14] In the data presented in this paper, debuccalization occurring outside the intervocalic environment is not observed. Yet, a more thorough examination of Leslau's extensive corpus shows that the process occurs in every environment and therefore must have occurred after the deglottalization process: /t' → ʔ/ in /ʔu ʷaʔɛ/ Ennemor /ʔu a ɛ/ Endegeny meaning 'narrow' and /k' → ʔ/ in /ʔinawɛ/ Ennemor /ʔɨ ɨw/ Endegeny meaning 'near'. This debuccalization is a large-scale merger where all ejectives (glottalized consonants) are becoming glottal stops.

4.2 Shared Innovations Linking Mesmes with PWG

Table 4.14. Guragoid and Mesmes Forms for 'moon(light)'

Gloss	Lexemes	Speech variety
moon(light)	t'ɛrrak': a	Muher
	t'ɛɾak' a	Desa
	t'anak' a	Gura
	t'ɛnak' a	Cheha
	t'anak' a	Gyeto
	t'ɛnnak': a	Ezha
	t'ɛnnak': a	Mesqan
	dɛrrak': a	Kistane
	danaʔ a	Ennemor
	danaʔ ɛ	Endegeny
	dɛnaʔ a	Mesmes

As in the example in table 4.13, we can trace the changes from the proposed proto-form in Outer South Ethiopic to the realization in Mesmes (table 4.15):

Table 4.15. The Relative Chronology as Evidenced in 'moon(light)'

Rules	*t'ɛrrak'a
1b.	*r > n
	t'ɛnnak'a
2.	*t' > t
	tɛnnak'a
3a.	*k' > ʔ
	tɛnnaʔa
3b.	*t > d
	dɛnnaʔa

The first sound change found in this example is the merger of liquids where *r > n when it is geminate, preconsonantal, or initial (Hetzron 1977).

This rule, like rule (1a), occurs in the CPWG group: 1b. *r > n in Gura, Ezha, Cheha, Gyeto, Ennemor, Endegeny, Mesmes (CPWG group).

The next two sound changes (deglottalization and debuccalization) have already been discussed. Deglottalization (2) is followed by debuccalization (3a). It must be noted that rule (1b) must precede rules (2) and (3) in time because of which lects it affects. It can further be assumed that rule (2) occurs before both (3a) and (3b). In (3b), after the initial consonant has been deglottalized, it undergoes the voicing rule /t/ → /d/ discussed in 4.2.1.

4.2.4 Additional links between Mesmes and PWG

There are a number of phonological processes which shed further light on the linguistic relationships internal to Peripheral West Gurage, including Mesmes. The details of some of these processes are discussed in the following subsections.

4.2.4.1 Weakening of the bilabial nasal and the genesis of the nonetymological /n/

The nongeminate bilabial nasal,[15] in intervocalic environments, appears to have already been weakened in PWG—or 'spirantized', to use Leslau's[16] terminology for the weak articulations of some Guragoid phones (1979). This process of weakening in such a highly sonorant position is not enough evidence to suggest shared history since such processes can happen independently in a variety of languages, regardless of genetic relationship. This sort of spirantization is too common cross-linguistically to use for subgrouping. Yet, it must also be argued that when viewed in the context of additional changes which are more indicative of shared history, these weakenings may help to confirm relationships internal to a particular subgroup.

Table 4.16 shows the weakening of nongeminate /m/ within PWG, as well as the later changes that have taken place in Mesmes. The /m/, in this intervocalic environment, even in the PWG proto-form, is already weakly articulated [m̯].[17] Both the Endegeny and Mesmes varieties share the same innovation of *m → /w/, both intervocalically and elsewhere,

---

[15] The *PWG geminate bilabial nasals do not weaken; an example can be seen in the word 'fat' (item 25 in appendix A).

[16] Leslau (1979, vol. 3:29). provides a discussion of spirantization/weakening.

[17] The "subscript corner" diacritic is the IPA notation for weak articulation in disordered speech (International Phonetic Association 1999:189, 193). Here, I am employing it for a weak articulation in standard speech.

4.2 Shared Innovations Linking Mesmes with PWG

as attested in items 2, 10, 14, and 48 in appendix A (but see item 9 for an exception, where final *m > /m/ in Endegeny).[18] That is, in those lexemes where the /m/ is seen to have weakened to the /w/ in Endegeny, the same forms show the innovation in Mesmes. 'Sun' (80) appears to be an exception to the rule. I would argue, however, that this example involves the nasal formation process where nasalized vowels are realized as oral vowels followed by nasal consonants in Mesmes. It appears that the /m/ is the result of the nasalized vowel and the /w/.[19] The presence of the *m in the proto-form is further supported by other South Ethiopic languages, as in the Amharic /amɛd/ 'ash.'

Table 4.16. Historical Derivation for Mesmes 'ashes'

	Lexemes	Speech variety
PWG Proto-form (#2)	* hamɛ̃ d*	
	amɛ̃ d	Gyeto
	amɛ̃ d	Ennemor
/m/ → /w/	awɛ̃ d	Endegeny
nasal formation	awɛnd	
addition of final V	hawɛnda	Mesmes

*The loss of the initial laryngeal /h/ (also found in wordlist items 10, 31, 61, 69, and 76) in all of Gurage except for Mesmes does not appear to be indicative of shared history. Rather, I take the loss of the laryngeal to be an areal phenomenon that swept across Gurage proper; Mesmes, not being part of Gurage geographically, was left unaffected. This account explains why the loss of the laryngeal does not correlate with the shared innovations discussed in this work.

In a few instances, the Mesmes form has lost even the /w/ trace of the bilabial and has resulted in a geminate vowel, a compensatory process (14, appendix A). Nongeminate /m/s which are part of a consonant cluster appear to be protected from weakening, their environment not being intervocalic (8 and 38).

---

[18] The voiced bilabial stop /b/ undergoes a similar process in Endegeny and Mesmes (#s 26 and 49).

[19] The verb 'to give' (31) does not show further weakening of the spirantized /m/ in PWG, and thus remains an unexplained exception.

A brief discussion concerning the changes internal to Mesmes is necessary before continuing the discussion of nasalization in PWG. The Mesmes form has undergone the innovation of a final vocalism (a detailed discussion follows in chapter 5) and the nasal formation process where nasalization on vowels (in many cases an innovation itself) in PWG often corresponds with the formation of a non-etymological nasal consonant in Mesmes.[20]

Table 4.17 provides another example. In this case, there is good evidence that the PWG proto-form did not have a nasal consonant or a nasal vowel. There is no evidence within other Gurage languages or in other South Ethiopic languages (such as Amharic) of the nasal that appears in the Mesmes form. Leslau offers the reconstruction /*t ' ifɨr/ for all of Gurage.

Table 4.17. Historical Derivation for Mesmes 'claw'

	Lexemes	Speech variety
PWG Proto-form (#13)	*t ' ifɨr	
	t ' ifɨr	Gyeto
debuccalization	ʔifɨr	
spontaneous nasalization	ʔĩ fɨr	Ennemor and Endegeny
vowel backing	ʔũfur	
nasal formation	ʔunfur	
loss of initial glottal	unfur	
addition of final V	unfura	Mesmes

Only the Endegeny and Ennemor forms have a nasalized vowel, according to Leslau (1979). In every example throughout the wordlist data in appendix A, Gyeto preserves any nasalization that is inherited from the PWG Proto form. Boivin (1996) provides evidence that spirantized nasals, which spread the [nasal] feature and, even more interesting, glottal stops, which are often remnants of "gutturals" (pharyngeals and laryngeals, in

---

[20] Apart from two exceptions, nasalization of vowels in Mesmes is dispreferred (see 10 in appendix A and lines 5 and 6 of the Mesmes text in appendix C for the exceptions).

4.2 Shared Innovations Linking Mesmes with PWG

this case), may lead to the genesis of a non-etymological /n/ in PWG.[21] Boivin writes:

#ħ/ʕ +V +C → #h/ʔ +Ṽ +C → #h/ʔ +V +n +C

> Let us first consider [the process above]. Aside from the change in the gutturals /ħ/→/h/ and /ʕ/→/ʔ/, the vowel V between the laryngeal /h/ or /ʔ/ and the consonant C first becomes nasalized. This nasalization then turns into a full nasal consonant /n/ (1996:23)

Boivin's conclusion is that nasalization is specified for the glottal in these languages. His argument is that the process is not merely articulatory (if it were, many languages should exhibit the same phenomenon) but cognitive (1996:33). Boivin, in his article, notes that in many cases, the nasalized vowel is maintained in Inor and a full nasal consonant is not yet formed. While the phenomenon is rare, the link between glottalic sounds and nasality, or *rhinoglottophilia*, as it has been termed (Matisoff 1975), is not completely unknown in other languages (Michailovsky 1975, Parker 1996 and Blust 1998).

The Mesmes wordlist and the relative chronology of the innovations in PWG offer some credence to Boivin's claims.[22] Table 4.16 shows the spirantized nasal spreading its feature and resulting in a non-etymological nasal consonant /n/ in Mesmes.[23] In this case, no laryngeal is involved. Table 4.17 shows that the glottal stop, even one resulting from the large-scale merger of glottalized consonants through debuccalization in PWG, can also trigger nasalization in Ennemor and Endegeny and the resulting non-etymological /n/ in Mesmes.

---

[21] Hetzron (1977) has also suggested that the non-etymological /n/ is a result of gutturals. Leslau (1992b) disagrees with Hetzron, suggesting that nasalization is also found in environments without gutturals.

[22] For a more complete discussion regarding spontaneous nasalization and rhinoglottophilia in Mesmes and the role of articulation and perception in the process, see Ahland (2006).

[23] The spirantized nasal in Mesmes also changes /*r/ → /n/ in those words where the nasal spread is not blocked by the presence of an obstruent (obstruents are specified for nasality). /*r/ becomes /n/ in wordlist examples 48, 79, and 95 through this process. In item 13, the spread is blocked by the obstruent /f/ and in 21, the spread is blocked by /z/. In item 37, the nasal is geminate and thus not spirantized. No spread is able to occur and thus the /r/ remains in Mesmes.

Table 4.18. Historical Derivation for Mesmes 'bird'

	Lexemes	Speech variety
PWG Proto-form (#6)	*ã : fʷ	
	ã : fʷ	Gyeto, Ennemor and Endegeny
nasal formation	a : nfʷ	
vowel backing through labialization spread	ɔ : nfʷ	
addition of final V and loss of labialization	ɔ : nfa	Mesmes

Table 4.18 shows the same process, but in this instance the nasalization is due to an ancient pharyngeal:

> That the debuccalized ejective produces nasalization is not a surprise, given that proto-glottal stops are able to accomplish the same. The PWG Proto-word for 'mouth' is *ãfʷ. In this case, the nasalization is attributable to a glottal stop, whose reflex is still found in the initial position on cognates in the Ethio-Semitic languages of Gi'iz, Tigre and Tigrinya ʔaf (Leslau 1979). The daughters of PWG exhibit the same nasalization: Ennemor ãfʷ; Endegeny ãfʷ (Leslau 1979); and Mesmes anfe (Bender 1971). This nasalization is also found in Cheha: ãf (Leslau 1979), but not outside of Gurage, as shown by the Amharic form: af (Ahland 2006)

The vowel on 'bird' is nasalized throughout the Gurage languages and can be assumed to have been inherited by PWG as a nasalized vowel (Leslau 1979). Again, as in the data in tables 4.16 and 4.17, the nasal consonant /n/ is unknown elsewhere in Ethio-Semitic, according to Leslau (1979, vol. 3:20).

Thus, the nasal formation process results in a non-etymological /n/ in Mesmes where nasalized vowels are found in Ennemor and Endegeny and sometimes Gyeto (depending on the source of nasalization).[24] The nasal-

---
[24] In those cases where debuccalization results in nasalization from the innovation of the glottal, Gyeto does not show any [nasal] feature.

4.2 Shared Innovations Linking Mesmes with PWG

ization may be due to the spreading of a nasal feature from a spirantized nasal consonant (wordlist #s 2 and 3), the historical presence of an ancient pharyngeal (wordlist #s 6, 54 and 60), or a glottal stop formed through debuccalization in the glottalized consonant merger found in Ennemor, Endegeny, and Mesmes (wordlist # 13). Ultimately, whatever the genesis of the nasalization and the non-etymological /n/, the fact remains that a systematic correspondence between Mesmes and other PWG languages exists.

4.2.4.2 Relevant vocalic length

The Peripheral West Gurage varieties share the innovation of phonemic vocalic length (Hetzron 1977 and Leslau 1992, 1996). Hetzron writes, "...PWG developed long vowels....They may represent older diphthongs (*moodä* 'he died' from **mawta*), but most often they result from the loss of an intervocalic consonant" (Hetzron 1977:36). Mesmes maintains the vocalic length in the same lexemes where it is found in other PWG varieties (wordlists #s 3, 6, 15, 24, 27, 48, 76, and 84). There are only two clear exceptions to this rule in the Mesmes wordlist (#s 17 and 96). The verb 'to go/to pass' (# 32 in the wordlist) is found in the Mesmes text (lines 12 and 16) with the long vowel, as expected.[25]

Mesmes also exhibits a tendency to lengthen vowels which are not long in the other PWG varieties: first, in a compensatory process where consonants are lost through *weakening* (wordlist #s 14, 44, 72, and 85) and second, in a similar process where inherited geminate consonants are reduced to single consonants and the vowel to the left of the proto geminate consonant is lengthened (#s 18, 42, 53, 61, 63, 64, 65, 88, and 90).

Table 4.19 provides an example of compensatory lengthening brought about by consonant loss in Mesmes. In this example, the glottal stop is lost intervocalically, leading to the long vowel in Mesmes.

---

[25] I am uncomfortable with the term "innovation" used to refer to all of the examples of vocalic length in PWG. In many cases, as Hetzron notes, the length is due to a compensatory process of consonant or glide loss. In a few instances, like /wɛ : r-'ɛ/ in line 12 of the Mesmes Text (appendix C), the vowel length is a true innovation and not attributable to any compensation.

Table 4.19. Historical Derivation for Mesmes 'three'

	Lexemes	Speech variety
PWG Proto-form (#85)	*soʔost	
	soʔost	Gyeto, Ennemor, and Endegeny
deletion of glottal	soost	
vowel laxing*	sɔ : st	
addition of final V	sɔ : sti	Mesmes

*In this case, the geminate vowels [oo] appear to have been interpreted as in a closed syllable. It is likely that the Mesmes vowels /ɔ/ and /ʊ/ have come about as a result of closed syllables, historically (see section 4.2.4.3).

There are many examples of the second process described above, where geminate consonants are reduced and the vowel undergoes lengthening as a result. The geminate consonants in the following charts are indeed attested in those geminating varieties (Ezha, in particular) outside of PWG (Leslau 1979). The process is limited to the coronal phonemes /j/, /t/, /ɲ/, and /n/:

Table 4.20. Historical Derivation for Mesmes 'rain (n)'

	Lexemes	Speech variety
PWG Proto-form (63)	*dijjɛ	
	dijɛ	Gyeto
	dijɛ	Ennemor
	dijɛ	Endegeny
vocalic lengthening	di : j	Mesmes

4.2 Shared Innovations Linking Mesmes with PWG

Table 4.21. Historical Derivation for Mesmes 'mountain'

	Lexemes	Speech variety
PWG Proto-form (53)	*aɲɲɛ	
	aɲɲɛ	Gyeto, Ennemor and Endegeny
vocalic lengthening	aːɲɛ	
assimilation of final V	aːɲa	Mesmes

Table 4.22. Historical Derivation for Mesmes 'one'

	Lexemes	Speech variety
PWG Proto-form (61)	*hatt	
	aːt	Gyeto
	at	Ennemor
	att	Endegeny
vocalic lengthening	aːt	
addition of final V	haːti	Mesmes

In the first case, in table 4.21, only Mesmes appears to reflect (through vocalic length) the proto-geminate consonant within PWG; as mentioned earlier, the length is attested in Ezha (Leslau 1979). In table 4.21, however, the other PWG varieties have not lost the length (that is, one of the consonants making up the geminate pair), yet Mesmes, again, shows the lengthening of the vowel. Table 4.22 shows that the process of gemination reduction in each of the PWG varieties appears not to be indicative of shared history but an independent process in each lect. In each instance, Mesmes exhibits vocalic lengthening. It must also be mentioned that this process can involve any form of gemination in PWG. For example, the second radical of verbs marked for perfect aspect is geminate in those Gurage languages which maintain gemination. The Mesmes wordlist item (42) /ɔːtɔɔ/ 'to kill' shows that, again, the geminate consonant may be reduced and the vowel lengthened as a result—even in the case where verb roots are involved.[26]

4.2.4.3 Other vocalic changes in Mesmes

In addition to lengthening, there are other vocalic changes internal to Mesmes. A careful examination of the comparative wordlists in appendix A shows the following correspondences: /ɛ/ in PWG and /ɔ/ in Mesmes (#s 4, 8, 9, 40, 57, 83, 87), /i/ in PWG and /ʊ/ in Mesmes (#s 13, 21, 74, 90, 95), /u/ in PWG and /ʊ/ in Mesmes (#s 37, 44, and 60), and /o/ in PWG and /ɔ/ in Mesmes (#s 71 and 85). In each of these examples, the change appears to have occurred within closed syllables in Mesmes. There are examples of such vocalic changes found in the Mesmes text as well (line 1 notes, appendix D).

Mesmes vowels exhibit a tendency to undergo a degree of neutralization in closed syllables, with PWG /ɛ/ and /o/ merging to /ɔ/ and PWG /i/ and /u/ merging to /ʊ/. While there are certainly exceptions[27] to this process, the tendency is well attested in Mesmes. It is likely that this merger is the historical process by which the vowels /ɔ/ and /ʊ/ have become phonemes in Mesmes. While these vowels are most frequently found in closed syllables, there are instances of them in open syllables as well.[28] It appears that an additional process has occurred where the velars /g/, /k/, and /w/ and /ʔ/ can bring about the /ɔ/ and /ʊ/. Out of all the open syllable instances of these two vowels, only three exceptions are not in close proximity to one of the three velars or to the glottal stop (wordlist #s 12, 19, and 31). It must also be mentioned that these vowels are not found in other Ethio-Semitic languages. They are in the Highland East

---

[26] Leslau argues that gemination in Endegeny is phonetically conditioned. In this case, the gemination is maintained because the verb ends in /r/, according to his analysis (Leslau 1992c). The Gurage root appears to be /qtl/ or /qt'l/—Leslau cites both (1979, volume 3:263). Rose offers an alternative analysis where gemination in Endegeny is determined by the duration of the final consonant: "if the final consonant is of short duration, gemination is found. If the final consonant is of long duration (i.e. a voiceless fricative or ejective), then no gemination is found" (Rose 2003:1).

[27] There are 6 exceptions where the vowels /i/, /o/, and /u/ are found in closed syllables: 24, 25, 30, 55, 75, and 93. Out of these, numbers 25 and 55 appear to be borrowings since they do not show participation in expected sound change processes: debuccalization and the non-etymological /n/ nasal formation process, respectively.

[28] For /ɔ/ in open syllables, see wordlist items 12, 19, 22, 31, 32, 38, 42, 51, 56, 73, and 77. For /ʊ/ in open syllables, see wordlist items 35, 84, and 92. It is not possible to trace the reason why the *i in item #90 underwent the vowel change. The change could be due to the closed syllable, before the loss of the /r/ or it could be due to the presence of the glottal stop.

4.2 Shared Innovations Linking Mesmes with PWG

Cushitic languages of Hadiyya and Kambaata, the two Cushitic languages which have had the most impact on Mesmes. This is discussed in more detail in section 5.5 of chapter 5 on externally-induced change.

As has been included in table 4.18, there are instances in the Mesmes data where labialization spreads and affects vowel quality, typically backing/rounding vowels to /ɔ/, /o/, and /u/.[29] Leslau (1992). and Hetzron (1977) note the same labialization spread affecting vowels in Ennemor and Endegeny as well. The Mesmes data also show some examples of vowel harmony involving the vowels /o/ and /ɔ/ (wordlist #s 12, 17, 32, 33, 42, and 73).[30] This sort of harmony involving back vowels is not found in other PWG languages nor in the Cushitic languages of Hadiyya and Kambaata (Hudson 1976 and Sim 1989).

4.2.4.4 Pharyngeal archaisms and systematic metathesis

Another interesting sound change involves the pharyngeal consonant in Ethio-Semitic. In many Ethio-Semitic languages, this consonant is lost today, and only the vowel that followed it, /a/, remains in most of Gurage: Cheha, Ezha, Muher, Gura, Kistane, Mesqan, and Desa. However, the Peripheral West lects have preserved the pharyngeal through maintaining the glottal stop preceding the vowel: /ʔɑ/.[31] This is not an innovation itself, since the glottal is most likely a retention of some of the pharyngeal's features.

There is still, however, a regular sound change process within Peripheral West Gurage, strengthening the evidence for the subgrouping.

---

[29] Examples of this phenomenon are found in table 4.18 and appendix D, notes on lines 5, 13, and 20.

[30] Wordlist items (45) and (51) also show duplication of the vowels /o/ and /ɔ/, respectively. Each of these words, however, ends with the final /a/; the harmony does not extend to all the vowels.

[31] Leslau refers to these glottal-consonant sequences as 'stop-attacks' in his writing (1992c:263).

Table 4.23. Pharyngeal Archaism in 'to hear'

Gloss	Lexemes	Speech variety
hear	sɛm a	Cheha
	semmɑ	Ezha
	sɛmmɑ	Muher
	sɛm ɑ	Gura
	sɛmmɑ	Kistane
	sɛmmɑ	Mesqan
	sɛm ɑ	Desa
	sɛmʔɑ	Gyeto
	sɛmʔɑ	Ennemor
	sɛpmɑ	Endegeny
	sɔʔmɑ	Mesmes

Leslau (1979) posits the Ethiopic etymon /*smH/ for the data in table 4.23. The final /a/ vowel in the data is the vowel which followed the *pharyngeal. The geminate /m/s are due to consistent gemination (in those geminating varieties of Gurage) in the derivational process which derives the perfect form of the verb. This is not due to any compensatory lengthening. As mentioned earlier, only some of the Gurage lects have maintained gemination as a relevant feature.

Within Peripheral West Gurage, both Endegeny and Mesmes have metathesized the glottal and the nasal.[32] In fact, this metathesis occurs regularly in the perfect.[33] There is no metathesis found in the jussive and imperfect forms of these verbs in Endegeny (Leslau 1992c). Table 4.24 provides another example of this process.

---

[32] I doubt the transcription of the Endegeny word here. The difference between [ʔm] and [pm] is very difficult to distinguish. Hetzron, also, questioned Leslau's transcription here (1977).

[33] Leslau labels this the /zɛtna/ pattern (1992c:463). The metathesis is not found in other tenses/aspects in Endegeny. It does appear that Mesmes has undergone some leveling. While the verb 'to marry' /(a)gɛppaʔa/ in Endegeny follows Leslau's /nɛssaʔa/ pattern, for those verbs "whose original third radical was /ʔ/ or /ʕ/ and whose second radical is a consonant other than n or m" (Leslau 1992c:464), the same verb in Mesmes follows the /zɛtna/ pattern, having undergone analogical leveling /gɛʔpa/ (line 7 of the Mesmes Text, appendix C).

4.2 Shared Innovations Linking Mesmes with PWG

Table 4.24. Pharyngeal Archaism in 'to eat'

Gloss	Lexemes	Speech variety
eat	bɛn ɑ	Cheha
	bɛnnɑ	Ezha
	bɛnnɑ	Muher
	bɛn ɑ	Gura
	bɛllɑ	Kistane
	bɛnnɑ	Mesqan
	bɜnnɑ	Desa
	bɛnʔɑ	Gyeto
	bɛmʔɑ	Ennemor
	bɛtnɑ	Endegeny
	bɑʔnɔː	Mesmes

In the case of table 4.24, Leslau posits the Ethiopic etymon /*blH/ (1979). Once again, the pharyngeal becomes the vowel /a/ in most cases, but /ʔɑ/ in the Peripheral West lects. Then the metathesis occurs in both Endegeny and Mesmes.

This metathesis does not have any relationship to the historical process of the pharyngeal becoming /ʔɑ/. Evidence for this claim is found in the case of 'twenty', in table 4.25, for which Leslau posits the Ethiopic root as /klʔ/ (1979). Thus, the glottal stop is not an innovation in PWG but a retention, and no pharyngeal is involved.

Table 4.25. Systematic Metathesis in Endegeny and Mesmes

Gloss	Lexemes	Speech variety
twenty	kʷɨja	Kistane
	xu ja/huja	Mesqan
	xʷɨja/xʷet as : ɨr	Muher
	xʷɨja	Cheha
	xʷɨjja	Ezha
	xʷɨjʔa	Gyeto
	xʷijʔa	Ennemor
	hu ʔjɛ	Endegeny
	hu ʔja	Mesmes

As a side note, the gemination in Ezha is, in this case, likely due to the loss of the glottal stop and could thus be considered compensatory. Again, the same metathesis process occurs in both Endegeny and Mesmes. This process of metathesis is so regular that it must have occurred at a time prior to the divergence of Endegeny and Mesmes, but, of course, after the split within PWG between Gyeto and Ennemor on the one hand and Mesmes and Endegeny on the other.[34]

Even a cursory examination of the morphological and syntactic retentions discussed in the early sections of this chapter provides sound argument for assuming Mesmes to be genetically related to the Gurage languages. More importantly, the plethora of shared innovations attested in the Mesmes and PWG pronominal paradigms and lexicons provide conclusive evidence that Mesmes did share some history with the PWG languages and with Endegeny in particular. A complete understanding of the Mesmes data is not possible without considering the apparent impact that the shift to Hadiyya has had on the Mesmes syntax, lexicon, and phonology. This is the subject of chapter 5.

---

[34] Chapter 5 includes an explanation for how these glottal stop-consonant complexes came about. It is likely that externally induced change is involved.

5

Evidence of Contact-Induced Change in the Mesmes Data

5.1 The Nature of Externally Induced Change

The Mesmes speech form is surrounded by the Cushitic language Hadiyya. As was shown in the second chapter, the Mesmes people have adopted Hadiyya as their language and have lost the ability to speak Mesmes. This language contact between Mesmes and Hadiyya and subsequent shift to the more socially and linguistically dominant Hadiyya language, coupled with the fact that Mesmes and other Gurage languages make up part of a convergence area (see table 2.1) marked by high degrees of multilingualism, suggests that the Mesmes speech form has likely undergone some degree of change as a result of contact. This is externally induced change.

Thomason and Kaufman charge, "The methodological principles embodied in the powerful Comparative Method include an assumption that virtually all language change arises through intrasystemic causes" (1988:1). Yet, as has already been asserted by other Ethio-Semitic and Guragoid scholars, there are indeed features in Gurage languages that have come about through contact (Hetzron 1977, Leslau 1945, 1979, 1992c, and 1992d). Thomason and Kaufman argue that this is, in fact, the norm in the world's languages, "We believe, with Schuchardt, Bailey, and

Mühlhäusler, that foreign interference in grammar as well as in lexicon is likely to have occurred in the histories of most languages" (1988:3).

The Mesmes corpus, made up of the text, wordlist, and unpublished grammatical paradigms, provides evidence that while much of the phonology, grammar, and lexicon appears to be inherited from the Proto-PWG parent. There are significant changes in Mesmes which correspond to structures found in the Cushitic languages of Hadiyya and neighboring Kambaata.

5.2 Loanwords in the Mesmes Wordlist

While lexical borrowing is not necessarily indicative of a high degree of bilingualism, it is certainly a contact-induced phenomenon. Perhaps of greatest interest is the seemingly very small number of non-Guragoid words in the Mesmes list and text. Only three[1] words in the wordlist appear to be from a non-Guragoid source (see appendix B for the Hadiyya/Kambaata wordlists): (29) /ta : ye/ 'fly' from Kambaata /tawi̱ /, (46) /fɔre/ 'liver' from Hadiyya /afɛre/, and (69) /-ha : ʲjɔ : -/ 'to see' from Amharic /aj : ɛ/.

The fact that there are not many loanwords in the Mesmes data may be suggestive of the speakers' history. Thomason and Kaufman argue that if language A speakers were learning to speak language B, then their mother tongue, language A, would have some impact on the phonology and structure of language B, though not the lexicon, necessarily:

> ...unlike borrowing, interference through imperfect learning does **not** begin with vocabulary: it begins instead with sounds and syntax, and sometimes includes morphology as well before words from the shifting group's original language appear in the [target language]. (1988:39; emphasis in original)

This is quite interesting, given that there is no evidence that Hadiyya-speaking peoples were ever learning Mesmes. However, since the area is marked by a high-degree of multilingualism, it is not difficult to entertain such possibilities. The mother-tongue Hadiyya speakers certainly were not in the process of shifting to the minority Mesmes language, but enough of them may have learned to speak the language that, at the time when Mesmes was in decline, the Hadiyya-influenced mispronunciations

---

[1] It must be noted that wordlist item #81 'to swim' is also found in Hadiyya and in Kambaata as well as in Gurage. The sound change of debuccalization of the glottalized consonant suggests that this word was inherited through normal transmission to Mesmes—even though it may originally be of Cushitic origin.

could have led to changes in the phonology and syntax, without necessarily affecting the Mesmes lexicon to any great extent. The Mesmes people would have also been speaking Hadiyya which may have made these phonological and syntactic changes more palatable.

5.3 Paradigmatic Leveling in Mesmes

In the pronominal paradigm (table 4.3 in section 4.2), the Mesmes data show an example of interlinguistic analogical leveling. Where Outer South Ethiopic languages all maintain gender distinctions in the plural forms (2nd masculine plural/2nd feminine plural and 3rd masculine plural/3rd feminine plural), Mesmes appears to have lost this distinction in both 2nd and 3rd persons. Hadiyya does not make these gender distinctions in plural forms and the loss of this feature in Mesmes may be considered due to a sort of interlinguistic analogy—a leveling between lects. That is, the Mesmes paradigm has been simplified on the pattern of the Hadiyya paradigm. Like Hadiyya, Mesmes does not make any distinction for gender in plural forms.

Table 5.1. Comparison of Mesmes and Hadiyya Pronominal Paradigms

	Mesmes	Hadiyya*
1 S	hijja	ani
2 M S	ahe	ati
2 F S	a : ʃe	ati
3 M S	hude	itʼo
3 F S	ʃi : di	isi
1 PL	inna	neese
2 M PL	ahu : we	ki ʔne
2 F PL	ahu : we	ki ʔne
3 M PL	hahunje	itʼu / issu
3 F PL	hahunje	itʼu / issu

*These Hadiyya data are from Hudson (1976).

However, Mesmes has maintained the gender distinction in the 2nd person singular while Hadiyya has not. Such asymmetry in contact-induced change is not unusual, as changes that are due to contact situations are quite often asystematic. In this particular case, markedness reduction may not be involved, though it is worth noting that cross-linguistically the distinction of gender in the plural forms is more marked than the distinction of gender in the singular.

5.4 The Mesmes Final Vocalism

The data in tables 4.7 through 4.9 above show that Mesmes consistently adds a final vowel to the end of each noun.[2] This is clearly an innovation and is likely a result of contact with Hadiyya. Stinson notes with regard to Hadiyya: "Nouns in isolation end in /–a/, /-e/, or /–o/. This may be considered an accusative suffix since it is retained (often as a voiceless vowel) in the accusative, but dropped in the nominative" (1976:150).

Hudson agrees that the "accusative is the absolute or citation form of the noun" (1976:253). He points out that in Hadiyya, these final vowels are case markings but that they are "generally lost in connected speech."[3] As has already been seen, Ethio-Semitic nouns do not necessarily end in vowels. Yet, in each case, the Mesmes lexemes do. It appears this is due to the influence of the Hadiyya word structure that Stinson and Hudson describe. The likely scenario would have been that Mesmes speakers, having become bilingual in Hadiyya and having begun the shift to Hadiyya, were accustomed to the final vocalism underlying Hadiyya word structure. This may also be not so much a process of borrowing as a process of interference from imperfect learning.[4]

The question must then be raised, how did this change in word structure take place? Appendix B offers both the Hadiyya and Kambaata wordlists for comparison with Mesmes. Before comparing Mesmes with these Cushitic languages, it is important to note which final vowels in Mesmes nouns are not found in PWG. Table 5.2 provides those examples of final vowels in Mesmes (in all form classes, not only nouns) which are not found in other Gurage languages. Also considered in table 5.2 is the possibility of a phonological link with one of the Highland East Cushitic languages spoken in the region. In addition to Hadiyya, Kambaata, too, exhibits the final vowel in citation form. An important question is whether

---

[2] The only exceptions to this process are numbers (24) /ɨ ː n/ 'eye' and (55) /ʃum/ 'name'.

[3] Sim (1988:79) agrees that the final vowel is lost in connected speech and only barely audible in normal speech before pauses.

[4] There is also the possibility that the interference came from imperfect learning of Mesmes by mother-tongue Hadiyya speakers (see Thomason and Kaufman 1988 for a discussion of interference through imperfect learning). This is suggested as a possibility to account for the apparent lack of Hadiyya loanwords in the Mesmes data.

5.4 The Mesmes Final Vocalism

or not the final vowels in Mesmes (mainly /-a/ and /-e/, with three /–i/ vowels and one /–o/ vowel) correspond to the final vowel of the word with the corresponding meaning in one of the Cushitic languages.

Table 5.2. Mesmes Final Vocalism and Correspondences with Hadiyya and Kambaata

Lexeme #	New Mesmes vowel	Phonological link with Hadiyya/Kambaata
2	-a	in H
4	-a	in K
6	-a	in both H and K
10	-a	in neither
13	-a	in both H and K
21	-a	in neither
26	-e	in neither
27	-e	in neither
30	-e	in neither
36	-a	in H
37	-e	in H
40	-a	in K
44	-a	in K
45	-a	in both H and K
48	-a	in H
49	-e	in neither
51	-a	in both H and K
54	-e	in H
56	-a	in neither
61	-i	in neither
66	-e	in neither
74	-e	in neither
75	-a	in both H and K
78	-e	in K
79	-a	in H
83	-a	in K
85	-i	in neither

87	-a	in K
88	-e	in H
90	-i	in neither
91	-o	in neither
96	-e	in neither
97	-e	in H

Table 5.3. Results of Final Vowel Comparisons Between Mesmes, Hadiyya and Kambaata

in Hadiyya	in Kambaata	in both H and K	in neither	Total
8	6	5	14	33

No consistent phonological correspondences can be seen linking the Mesmes final vowels with corresponding words in either Hadiyya or Kambaata. In fact, 14 of the 33 'new' final vowels are of a different shape altogether from what is found in either Hadiyya or Kambaata.

A phonological explanation for the various shapes of the final vowel must be considered. The shapes /-a/, /-e/, and /-o/ are found in Hadiyya (Stinson 1976). In the Mesmes data, the vast majority of the examples (29 out of the 33) are either /-a/ or /-e/. Of the three /-i/ examples, each is a numeral (lexemes 61, 85, and 90).[5] It is by no means inconceivable that numerals would be treated in a different manner from the rest of the lexicon.

The only other example of a vowel other than /-a/ or /-e/ is the /-o/ in lexeme number 91. First, it should be pointed out that the /-o/ is not the final segment in the word; it is followed by an approximant: /maʔoj-/. The /-o/ is considered final only in the sense that it follows the final consonant found in the cognate forms elsewhere in Peripheral West Gurage (appendix A). It is possible that the glottal stop has had some impact on the original vowel here, but it is impossible to say for certain with only a single example in the data. For the present, the final /-o/ must be considered the lone example of its shape, as it is not predictable from any other process.

---

[5] Lexeme number 34 /saʔari/ 'grass', while ending with the /-i/ vowel, may be a retention of the final /-i/ found in Tigrinya and an even more ancient source, Akkadian (Leslau 1979). This vowel shape, as a result of contact with Hadiyya, is otherwise found only on numerals. Identical innovations of this final vowel /-i/ in Akkadian, Tigrinya, and Mesmes are not likely to be unrelated. As discussed earlier, the Gurage languages do, at times, maintain archaisms that are typically lost elsewhere in Semitic (see section 1.5).

There is a tendency in these data suggesting that Mesmes may have begun to harmonize its final vowel with the vowels in the stem. While the final vowel /-e/ is found attached with stems containing vowels that are either back or non-back, the /-a/ final vowel is found almost exclusively attached only to stems with back vowels. It may be that Mesmes initially added only the /-e/ as a final vowel, on the pattern of Hadiyya word structure.[6] After the addition of the vowel, a harmony process could have begun where stems with back vowels would require their final /-e/ to become /-a/ to agree in backness.

Since this kind of interference would only happen in cases of significant bilingualism, it is likely that the addition of the final vowel would have occurred late and thus the harmony process (which would have begun after the addition of the final vowel and not as interference from Hadiyya) was not able to complete and regularize before normal transmission was stopped. That is, the Mesmes language may have died before the vowel harmony could spread throughout the lexicon.

This very tentative solution would suggest that Mesmes, rather than indiscriminately adding various vowel shapes to the ends of words, copied the Hadiyya word structure by simply adding the /-e/ vowel word-finally. Then, processes of harmony and possibly even the creation of a numeral class were begun. Ultimately, however, there is not enough evidence to say for certain.

5.5 Vocalic Phenomena in Mesmes

The presence of lengthened vowels (section 4.2.4.2 above) in Peripheral West Gurage is also an innovation, most probably due to contact with Hadiyya. In Ethio-Semitic languages, lengthened vowels are generally not found. In Hadiyya, however, each of the five phonemic vowels has a relevant [+ long] counterpart (Stinson 1976). Recall that geographically, it is the Peripheral West languages (Gyeto, Ennemor, and Endegeny) that have the most contact with Hadiyya. Mesmes, of course, would be included in this grouping. While, as mentioned previously, the source of vocalic length in PWG and Mesmes can be identified as corresponding to diphthongs and compensatory lengthening through consonant loss (Hetzron 1977:36), it is likely that the presence of Hadiyya long vowels

---

[6] It is noted, of course, that Hadiyya has final vowels in addition to /-e/. My suggestion here is that Mesmes may have added the final vowel /-e/ without regard for the particular qualities of final vowels in Hadiyya. This would be a borrowing of word structure itself, not of particular vowels.

played a role in these long vowels reaching productive phonemic status in PWG, including Mesmes.

The merger of the /ɛ/ and /o/ neutralizing to /ɔ/ and the /ɨ/ and /u/ neutralizing to /ʊ/ (discussed in section 4.2.4.3) is likely also a result of contact with Hadiyya (and possibly other Highland East Cushitic languages). Hudson writes:

> In four of the languages [Higland East Cushitic], all but Sidamo, there is vowel laxing in closed syllables, and in the interior of words. This usually involves /a/ and /i/, less commonly /e/, and rarely /o/ and /u/. The lax allophones are, respectively, [ə, ɪ, ɛ, ɔ, ʊ]. (1976:249)

As mentioned in chapter four, it is likely that the Mesmes vowels /o/ and /u/ became /ɔ/ and /ʊ/, respectively, in closed syllables, on the pattern of Hadiyya phonology. The merger of /ɛ/ with /o/ and /ɨ/ with /u/ would have occurred later. Unlike Hadiyya and other Highland East Cushitic languages, additional processes involving velar consonants and the glottal stop/glottalization feature appear to have extended the distribution of /ɔ/ and /ʊ/, even to word-final positions (appendices A and B, #s 12, 19, 22, 32, 73, 77 and 84).

5.6 Possible Syntactic Change as a Result of Contact

Finally, there is a possible example of contact phenomena evident in Bender's unpublished data. Table 5.4 compares the bound possessive forms in Mesmes, Endegeny and Ennemor.[7]

---

[7] The Ennemor and Endegeny data are from Leslau (1979).

5.6 Possible Syntactic Change as a Result of Contact

Table 5.4. Bound Possessives in Mesmes, Endegeny, and Ennemor Attaching to 'house'

Gloss	Mesmes	Endegeny	Ennemor
1 S POSS	hī(ne)- bi : de	bi : d -iɲɛ	bi : d -iɲa
1 PL POSS	hiʔne- bi : de	bi : d -nijɛ	bi : d -inɨra
2 M S POSS	hɑhe- bi : de	bi : d -ɑhɛ	bi : d -ɑxɛ
2 M PL POSS	hɑho- bi : de	bi : d -ɑhu : j	bi : d -ɑxɨwa
2 F S POSS	haʃi : n- bi : de	bi : d -aʃ/-a : ʃi	bi : d -aʃ/-a : ʃa
2 F PL POSS	hɑho- bi : de	bi : d -ɑha : j	bi : d -ɑxa :
3 M S POSS	hudʊn- bi : de	(no bound form)	bi : d -xʷɛ
3 M PL POSS	hunu(j)e- bi : de	bi : d -heno :	bi : d -xɨnowa
3 F S POSS	ʃidi- bi : de	bi : d -ɛʃidaj /iʃɛ	bi : d -ʃa
3 F PL POSS	hunu(j)e- bi : de	(no bound form)	bi : d -xɨna :

Within the data, the same sorts of sound changes which have been seen elsewhere in the data are found—particularly those changes found in the pronominal paradigm (table 4.3). The position of the bound possessive form in Mesmes, however, is quite unexpected. In Ethio-Semitic languages, bound possessive pronominals always attach to the right of the stem, never to the left. The shapes of the prefixed elements in Mesmes are clearly Gurage, attesting to the same sound correspondences found in the pronominal paradigm. Yet the syntactic placement of these morphemes has shifted.

As has already been established, the contact between Mesmes and Hadiyya has had a noticeable impact on the structure of Mesmes words. Might it also have had an impact on Mesmes syntactic structure?

Table 5.5. Comparison of Mesmes and Hadiyya Bound Possessive Prefixes*

	Mesmes	Hadiyya
1 S POSS	hĭ(ne)-	i-
1 PL POSS	hɨʔne-	ni-
2 M S POSS	hɑhe-	ki-
2 M PL POSS	hɑho-	kiʔn-
2 F S POSS	hɑʃi : n-	ki-
2 F PL POSS	hɑho-	kiʔn-
3 M S POSS	hudʊn-	it ' : - / it '-
3 M PL POSS	hunu(j)e-	it ' : u- is : u-
3 F S POSS	ʃidi-	is-
3 F PL POSS	hunu(j)e-	it ' : u- / is : u-

*The Hadiyya data are from Hudson 1976.

An examination of the data above (table 5.5) shows that while the shape of the prefixal element in Mesmes is Guragoid, the syntactic placement suggests influence from Hadiyya. According to Hudson, both Hadiyya and Burji (another geographically distant Highland East Cushitic language) exhibit these prefixed possessives (Hudson 1976). Since this syntactic placement is unknown in any other Ethio-Semitic language and since it has already been established that contact with Hadiyya has worked to shape Mesmes, it follows that Hadiyya syntactic order could also have had an impact on Mesmes. This is especially true given the high degree of bilingualism in Hadiyya among Mesmes speakers at the time that Bender gathered his data.[8]

It must be admitted, however, that the Mesmes forms in table 5.4 may not actually be bound. The free form pronoun, with the prefixal genitive 'of' attached, would occur in the position before the possessed noun in an Ethio-Semitic language. A major challenge to this interpretation, however, is that the preposition-genitive marker in Ennemor is /ɛ-/ (Hetzron 1977:59). Something similar to this would be expected in Mesmes. However, the only consistent addition to these bound forms from the free forms in table 4.3 is that of the /h-/ in all but the 3rd feminine singular form.[9] Another challenge to the possibility of syntactic change

---

[8] It was likely that Mesmes was already moribund in 1969, given the lack of speakers today.

[9] The /h-/ is already present on the free forms in the 1st singular, the 3 masculine forms, and the 3rd feminine plural.

is that the Mesmes text does exhibit many examples of the 1S bound possessor, and in each case the possessor is an enclitic only (lines 1, 2, 4, 7, 8, 9, and 19). That is, in the Mesmes text, the bound possessive attaches to the right of the stem.

It is entirely possible that Bender and Stinson's Mesmes contact may have been more of a semi-speaker than Abegaz, the speaker from whom the text was collected. It could be that Abegaz's speech more closely resembles the original inherited Mesmes syntax and that Bender and Stinson's contact's speech had undergone more interference from Hadiyya.[10]

5.7 Cushitic *Stop-Attacks* in Endegeny and Mesmes

The glottal stop-obstruent complex segments discussed in section 4.2.4.4 are most probably of Cushitic origin (Leslau 1979, 1992d and Hetzron 1977). Hudson (1976), Hetzron (1977), and Leslau (1979) all mention the prevalence of glottal stop-sonorant sequences (considered complex segments in the Highland East Cushitic languages) found in Hadiyya and elsewhere in Cushitic. In fact, Leslau attributes these glottal stop-consonant complex segments in Endegeny to borrowings from the Highland East Cushitic languages: Hadiyya and Kambaata, among others (Leslau 1992d).[11]

I suspect that the metathesis found in Endegeny and Mesmes (discussed in section 4.2.4.4) is due to a remodeling on the basis of the Hadiyya complex segments. In Ennemor and Gyeto, the sonorants (/m/, /n/, and /j/ in tables 4.23, 4.24, and 4.25, respectively) precede the glottal, which is a partial reflex of the ancient pharyngeal. In Endegeny and Mesmes, a systematic metathesis is found, with the stop preceding the sonorant, exactly as occurs in Hadiyya.

Within Hadiyya, stop-sonorant complex segments are very common. In a convergence situation where there exists a high degree of multilectalism, contact-induced metathesis can be expected. If Mesmes and Endegeny speakers (prior to their divergence) were also commonly speaking Hadiyya, they might have found the sonorant followed by the glottal and then the vowel /a/ to be rather strange. It is likely that the metathesis occurred as a result of a re-patterning of the sequence (causing

---

[10] Sections 3.4 and 3.5 provide a discussion of different degrees of semi-speakers which may be encountered.

[11] The reader will recall that Leslau did not deal with Mesmes data in his work. Thus, he finds the glottal stop and consonant complex segments only in Endegeny and occasionally in Ennemor and Gyeto (Leslau 1992d:263).

metathesis) on the basis of Hadiyya's phonological template: something akin to an inter-linguistic process of proportional analogy. The metathesis could also be a change brought into PWG through the imperfect learning of Hadiyya speakers who were picking up these Gurage lects.

When the data are viewed holistically, they suggest that Mesmes has undergone interference from the Hadiyya language. Despite a dearth of loanwords, there remain several clear cases of structural interference: paradigmatic leveling of gender distinction in the pronouns, the addition of final vocalisms to word structure, new phonological processes such as the so-called vowel laxing in closed syllables, and the systematic metathesis leading to glottal stop-sonorant segments all point to outside interference. Without recourse to externally-induced language change, understanding of the Mesmes data would be limited at best and the data quite possibly misinterpreted.

6

Conclusion

6.1 Subgrouping Internal to PWG

It is clear from the examination of the syntax, morphology, and lexicon, as attested in Bender and Stinson's Mesmes data (both the wordlist and the unpublished pronominal paradigms) and in the Mesmes text, that Mesmes belongs to the Ethio-Semitic family and, even more specifically, the Western Gurage (CPWG group) cluster of languages. A more in-depth analysis of the sound changes consistently shows Mesmes to be a part of Hetzron's Peripheral West Gurage subgroup.

It is possible to examine the sound changes according to their relative depths in time. Table 6.1 shows the sound changes discussed in chapter 4. The numerals denote the relative time-depth of the innovation. For instance, in time-depth one, there are two sound changes l > r and r > n.[1] These changes occur in all the so-called CPWG varieties. The innovations at time-depth two, however, occur only in the Gyeto, Ennemor, Endegeny, and Mesmes varieties. Map 6.1 shows the geographic area pertaining to each of the sound changes in table 6.1:

---

[1] For the sake of space, the conditioning environments have not been included with these changes (the reader should see 4.2.3 for the environments).

Table 6.1. Sound Change at Relative Time-Depths

	Sound Change	Varieties attesting to the change
1a	l > r	Gura, Ezha, Cheha, Gyeto, Ennemor, Endegeny and Mesmes (CPWG)
1b	r > n	Gura, Ezha, Cheha, Gyeto, Ennemor, Endegeny and Mesmes (CPWG)
2a	dd > t	Gyeto, Ennemor, Endegeny and Mesmes (PWG)
2b	bb > p	Gyeto, Ennemor, Endegeny and Mesmes (PWG)
3a	x^j > ʃ	Ennemor, Endegeny and Mesmes (Inor)
3b	C' > C / #__V(C)(V)C'	Ennemor, Endegeny and Mesmes (Inor)
4a	C' > ʔ	Ennemor, Endegeny and Mesmes (Inor)
4b	ʔv > ʔṽ/vn	Ennemor, Endegeny and Mesmes (Inor)
4c	t > d	Ennemor, Endegeny and Mesmes (Inor)
5a	x > h	Endegeny and Mesmes (South Inor)
5b	m > w /V__V	Endegeny and Mesmes (South Inor)
5c	Nʔ > ʔN	Endegeny and Mesmes (South Inor)

6.1 Subgrouping Internal to PWG

Map 6.1. Geography and Sound Change

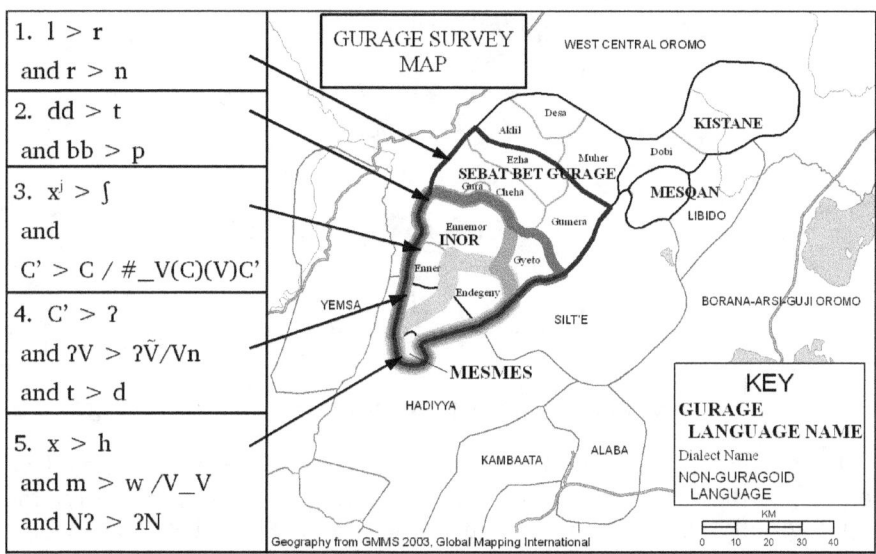

The early sound changes (1) occur in all of Hetzron's Central West and Peripheral West Gurage (including Mesmes). The sound changes in (2) occur throughout Peripheral West Gurage (including Mesmes). Time-depths (3) and (4) involve changes in the varieties of Ennemor, Endegeny, Enner and Mesmes.[2] Finally, the changes in time-depth (5) involve only the varieties of Mesmes and Endegeny.

Based on these data, it is possible to further subdivide Peripheral West Gurage, showing the relative relationship between the speech varieties on the basis of the patterns of sound change:

---

[2] It should be noted in this case that Gyeto is not included in the changes at time-depths 3 and 4. Rather, these depths help to explain the Gurage language survey's identification of *Inor* as a center of communication distinct from PWG (section 1.3). PWG includes Gyeto and the lects of Inor. According to the sound changes shown above, Inor must include Mesmes along with Enner, Ennemor, and Endegeny. In terms of intelligibility, however, Mesmes, as a result of the contact-induced changes discussed in chapter 5, is less intelligible with Endegeny than the other varieties of Inor are with one another (see 6.2).

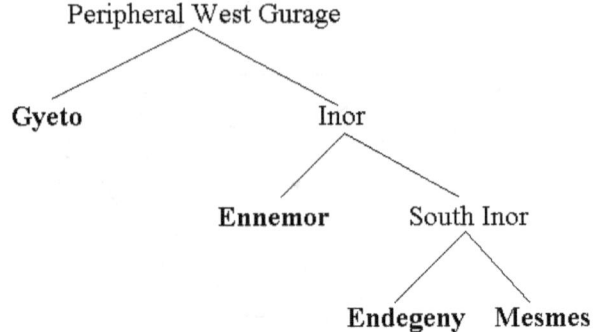

Figure 6.1. Proposed Subgrouping for Peripheral West Gurage.

For the subgroup within PWG that does not include Gyeto, I have elected to use the term *Inor* in keeping with the over-arching name for the intelligibility-based language boundaries proposed in 1.3. The specific subgroups in map 6.1 are not meant to suggest language boundaries but to show the history of the varieties. While Endegeny and Ennemor share a high degree of intelligibility with one another (table 1.1) and may be considered a single language in terms of intelligibility, there are innovations shared between Endegeny and Mesmes that are not found in Ennemor. The tree in figure 6.1 shows this historical relationship.[3] Likewise, while the intelligibility level between Mesmes and Endegeny is less than that between Endegeny and Ennemor, Mesmes and Endegeny do subgroup together, according to the shared innovations.

It must be argued that while there is certainly a relationship between intelligibility and shared history and while a positive correlation would normally be expected, the sorts of innovations which occur in particular lects and the nature of any externally-induced change and linguistic interference may have a negative impact on the level of intelligibility between varieties.[4] The relatively low comprehension score of Endegeny speakers on the Mesmes text (78 percent) is due in part to the contact phenomena discussed in chapter 5.[5] The five words in the Mesmes text

---

[3] The use of the term "South Inor" is meant to suggest the shared intelligibility of all of Inor as well as to note the geographic position of both Mesmes and Endegeny with reference to the other PWG lects.

[4] Bailey (1996) discusses the role of sound change and intelligibility.

[5] Grimes (1995) discusses an optimization methodology for determining language boundaries based on comprehension test scores.

which are unique to Mesmes are likely not enough to significantly reduce comprehension scores, especially since none of the ten questions in the comprehension test directly tested any of these words.

It should also be noted that Gyeto, as Hetzron (1972 and 1977) indicates, does not participate in all the innovations of Inor. The subgrouping in figure 6.1 reflects this fact. The details discussed in chapter 4 show that Gyeto does not participate in debuccalization, deglottalization, the /t/ → /d/ voicing or the /x^j/ → /ʃ/ change. Gyeto does, however, exhibit participation in the PWG innovations which led to lengthened vowels, the devoicing of /dd/ → /t/ and /bb/ → /p/ in the obstruent chain shift and vowel nasalization processes, where the vowel nasalization is due to spreading from weakly articulated nasal consonants (table 4.16) or from the effects of a glottal or pharyngeal through the relationship called *rhinoglottophilia* (table 4.18).[6] The syntactic, morphological, and lexical evidence also show Gyeto to be part of PWG (Hetzron 1977 and table 4.2).

6.2 Underscoring the Holistic Approach

As is clear from chapters 4 and 5, the Mesmes data are not fully elucidated until factors involving the linguistic history of the language and factors involving the social history of the people are considered. Without an examination of the externally induced changes that have taken place in Mesmes, the language would not appear to be so closely related to Endegeny. In fact, the changes in the vowels (the so-called laxed vowels) and the word structure (the final vocalism) could be enough to mask Mesmes' genetic position to the casual observer who is not familiar with the sound changes.

An examination of the externally induced changes and the reconstructed social history between the groups is also important because it aids in explaining why Endegeny speakers understood Mesmes less than they understood Ennemor (table 1.1) despite the fact that Mesmes and Endegeny appear to have shared history in which Ennemor does not participate.

While it is no longer spoken today, Mesmes still serves as an excellent source of comparative information which helps to cast light on the history of Endegeny in particular, and Gurage in general. The systematic

---

[6] Gyeto does not participate as frequently as the Inor lects in the nasalization since debuccalization (which does not occur in Gyeto but does occur in Endegeny, Ennemor, and Mesmes) does not feed the process in Gyeto—the reader should compare table 4.17, where debuccalization feeds nasalization through rhinoglottophilia, and table 4.18, where the nasalization is likely the result of an ancient guttural, not fed by debuccalization.

metathesis of the glottal stop and sonorant sequences in Endegeny, for example, is clearly seen to be a consistent process once the Mesmes data are added to the comparative pool. The Mesmes data also provide an interesting look at the sorts of contact-induced changes occurring when languages undergo a rapid shift and death: changes affecting both the phonology and morphology while leaving much of the syntax intact.

According to Hans-Jurgen Sasse (1992), half of the world's languages have become extinct in the last 500 years. In Africa alone, nearly 200 are on the endangered list (Sasse 1992). It is imperative that linguists make documentation of these disappearing speech forms a high priority and that languages like Mesmes be described before they are lost permanently.

Appendix A

Peripheral West Gurage Wordlist Comparison with Mesmes

Peripheral West Gurage Wordlist Comparison with Mesmes

#	Gloss	Mesmes	Endegeny	Ennemor	Gyeto	PWG Proto form
1.	all	ɔtˈtɛmi	itni / hinni	inni / itni	itni / inʔi	*iʔni / inni
2.	ashes	hawɛnda	awẽd	amẽd	amẽd	*hamẽd
3.	bark (tree)	ha : nna	ha : nɛ	xã : ra	xa : ra	*xa : na
4.	belly	kɔssa	kɛs	kɛs	dɛn	*kɛs
5.	big	kʼɔkʼɔ	nuʔ	nuʔ	nikʼ	*nikʼ
6.	bird	ɔ : nfa	ã : fʷ	ã : fʷ	ã : fʷ	*ã : fʷ
7.	bite (v)	ˈnakɔse	nɛkɛsɛ	nɛkɛsɛ	nɛkɛsɛ	*nɛkɛsɛ
8.	black (person/object in M & End. cattle in Enn. & Gyeto)	gɔmbɔnna	gɛmbɛnɛ	gɛmbɛnɛ	gɛmbɛnɛ	*gɛmbɛnnɛ
9.	blood	dɔ	dɛm	dɛm	dɛm	*dɛm
10.	bone	hãu̯wa	aʔiw	aʔim	atʼim	*hatʼim
11.	breast	tʼuwiye	tʼu / tʼiw	tʼu	tʼu	*tʼiwiyɛ
12.	burn (tr. v)	totosɔ	(a)tɛkɛsɛ	tɛkɛsɛ	tɛkɛsɛ	*tɛkɛsɛ
13.	claw	ʊnfura	ʔifir	ʔifir	tʼifir	*tʼifir
14.	cloud	do : na	dawɛnɛ	damẽra	damɛra	*damɛra
15.	cold (adj)	zi : z- ə	zizɛ	ziza	zi : za	*zi : za

Appendix A

16.	come	-mmaʔa	maʔa	maʔa	tʃaɲa	*matʼa / mɛtʼa
17.	die	mɔtɔ-	mo : dɛ	mo : dɛ	mo : tɛ	*mo : tɛ
18.	dog	gi : je	gɨjɛ	gɨjɛ	gɨjɛ	*gɨjjɛ
19.	drink (v)	sɛ͡tʃɔ	sɛt͡ʃʃʼɛ	sɛt͡ʃʼɛ	sɛt͡ʃʼɛ	*sɛt͡ʃʃʼɛ
20.	dry (adj)	dɛˈro- e	dɛrɛʔ	dɛrɛʔ	tʼɛrɛkʼ	*tʼɛrɛkʼ
21.	ear	ʊnˈzu : ra	ɨnzɨr	ɨnzɨr	ɨnzɨr	*ɨnzɨr
22.	eat	baʔˈnɔ :	bɛtna	bɛnʔa	bɛnʔa	*bɛnʔa
23.	egg	kʼu : ra	ɨnkʼulɛ	ɨnkʼura	ɨnkʼura	*ɨnkʼura
24.	eye	ɨ : n	e : n	ẽ : r	ajn	*e : n
25.	fat (n)	t͡ʃomma	t͡ʃo : mɛ	sɨwʔɛ	sɨwʔɛ	*t͡ʃomma *sɨwʔɛ
26.	father	a : we	aw	ab	ab	*ab
27.	fire	ɨˈsa : de	ɨsa : d	ɨsa : d	ɨsa : t / ɨsa : t	*ɨsa : t
28.	fish (n)	---	---	---	---	---
29.	fly (n)	ta : je	zɨmb	zɨmb	zɨmb	*zɨmb
30.	foot	ɨgˈgɨre	ɛgɨr	ɛgɨr	ɛgɨr	*ɛgɨr
31.	give	haˈmɔ-	amɛ	amẽ	aβɛ / amɛ	*hamɛ
32.	go	hɔˈrɔ : -	wɛ : rɛ	wɛ : rɛ	wɛ : rɛ	*wɛ : re
33.	good	moˈʔo	muʔ / ke : r	moʔ / ke : r	ke : r	*ke : r *mvcʼ
34.	grass	saʔari	saʔar	saʔar	sɛʔɛr	*sɛʔɛr

35.	hair ('of head' in M 'of body' in other PWG)	duˈgʊ : ra	dɨgɛr	dɨgɛr	dɨgɛr	*dɨgɛr
36.	hand	idʒdʒa	ɛdʒ	ɛdʒ	ɛdʒ	*ɛdʒ
37.	head	gʊnnure	gutnor	gunʔɛr	gunʔɛr	*gunnɛr
38.	hear	sɔˈʔma	sɛpma	sɛmʔa	sɛmʔa	*sɛmʔa
39.	heart	nu : ba	hin	xˈin	xˈin	*xˈin
40.	horn	kɔnna	kʼɛn	kʼɛn	kʼɛn	*kʼɛnn
41.	I	hijˈja	ɨjɛ	ɨja	ɨja	*ɨjja
42.	kill	ɔ : tɔrɔ	ʔɛttɛrɛ	ʔɛtɛrɛ / ʔetɛrɛ	kʼɛtʼɛrɛ	*kʼɛttʼɛrɛ
43.	know	haˈro : -	harɛ	xarɛ	xarɛ / harɛ	*xarɛ
44.	knee	gʊnno : da	guno : d	gurmẽd	gʷɨrmẽt	*gʷɨrmẽt
45.	leaf	koˈʔora	kɛʔɛr	kʼɨtʼɛr	kʼɨtʼɛr	*kʼɨtʼɛr
46.	liver	fɔre	hɛrt	xɛrt	xɛrt	*xɛrt
47.	long	gʊdˈdɔr-	fatʼu : lɛ	fatʼu : ra	fatʼu : ra	*fatʼura
48.	louse	kʼuˈwa : na	ʔɨwa : n	ʔɨ̃ma : r	kʼɨma : r	*kʼɨma : r
49.	man	sɛwʲe	sɛw	sɛb	sɛb	*sɛb
50.	many	kʼokʼo	dɨbaʃɛ	dɨbaʃɛ	dɨbaʃɛ	*dɨbaʃɛ
51.	meat	bɔˈsɔra	bɛsɛr	bɛsɛr	bɛsɛr	*bɛsɛr

Appendix A

52.	moon ('moonlight' in PWG)	dɛnˈnaʔa	dannaʔɛ	danaʔa	t'anak'a	*t'annak'a
53.	mountain ('hill' in Enn / Gyeto)	a : nja	aɲɲɛ	ʔaɲɛ	aɲɛ	*aɲɲɛ
54.	mouth	anfe	ãfʷ	ãfʷ	ãfʷ	*ãfʷ
55.	name	ʃum	ʃũ	ʃũ	ʃũ	*ʃum
56.	neck	angɔda	angɛd	angɛd	angɛt	*angɛt
57.	new	wɔjˈjamo	wɛjɛ	wɛja	gɛdɛr	*gɛdɛr *wɛja (after Gyeto split)
58.	night	haʷɔnʃɔde	massakkɛ	misaʔarɛ	misaʔarɛ	*misaʔarɛ
59.	---	---	---	---	---	---
60.	nose	anˈfʊnna	ãfunɛ	ãfuna	ãfuna	*ãfunna
61.	one	ha : ti	att	at	a : t	*hatt
62.	other	gɛnˈnamune	ɛɲɲɛ	eɲa	ingʷɛd	*ɛɲɲa *ingʷɛd
63.	rain (n)	di : je	dijɛ	dijɛ	dijɛ	*dijjɛ
64.	red	bi : ʃa	buʃɛ	biʃa	biʃa	*biʃʃa
65.	road	mo : ja	mejɛ	meja	mɛja	*mɛjja
66.	root ('bottom of thing' in End & Gyeto)	k'ine	ʔin	ɛsɨr	k'in	*k'in

67.	sand	t'o : na	aʃawɛ	aʃawa	aʃawa	*aʃawa
68.	say	-beɲɔ : -*	barɛ	barɛ	barɛ	*barɛ
69.	see	-ha : ʲjɔ : -	aʃʃɛ	aʃɛ	aʃɛ	*haʃʃɛ
70.	seed	zur(i)ji	zitnɛ / zɛr	ziɲʔɛ	ziɲʔɛ / zɛr	*ziɲʔɛ / *zɛr
71.	sit	-t͡ʃɔna : -	t͡ʃɛnna :	t͡ʃɛna :	t͡ʃo : na	*t͡ʃonna
72.	skin (human)	go : ga	gogɛ	gõ : dʒɛ	go : ga / gɛwɛdʒɛ	*gɛmɛdʒɛ
73.	sleep (v) ('sleep (n)' in PWG)	-wɔdɔ(ʔɔ)-	wɛ̃ʔɛ̃d	wiʔĩd	wiʔint	*wiʔint
74.	small	ʊ : nse	ons	ins	ɨrs	*ɨrs / *ins
75.	smoke (n)	tonna	tɛn	tɛn	tɛn	*tɛnn
76.	snake	hawa : j	ɛwa : w	(ɛ)saʔar tʃirɛ	((ɛ)saʔar) tʃirɛ	*tʃirɛ / *hɛwa : w
77.	stand	-tɛʃekkɔ-	(tɛ)ʃekkɛ :	(tɛ)ʃekɛβɛ	(tɛ)ʃekɛβɛ	*tɛʃekkɛβɛ
78.	star	hõhõje	hoho	xoxo / xoxowɛ	xoxẽm	*xoxomɛ
79.	stone	oṵna	ɛwɨn	ĩmɨ̃r	ɨmɨ̃r	*ɨmɨ̃r
80.	sun	ime :	ĩwã : jɛ / ajɛd	ũwã : jẽ / ajɛ : d	ẽwajɛ / ajɛt	*ima : jɛ / *ajɛ : d
81.	swim	-waʔa :	dara : gɛ	daragʹɛ	daragʹɛ	*dara : gɛ
82.	tail	dʒuʔe	dʒũwɛ	dʒĩwɛ	dʒĩwɛ	*dʒĩwɛ
83.	thin	k'ɔt͡ʃt͡ʃɨna	k'ɛt͡ʃt͡ʃɨr	k'ɛt͡ʃɨr	k'ɛt͡ʃɨr	*k'ɛt͡ʃt͡ʃɨr

Appendix A

84.	this	wʊ : -	wɑ	wɑ :	zɨ	*wɑ : *zɨ
85.	three	sɔ : sti	soʔost	soʔost	soʔost	*soʔost
86.	you (m.sg.)	ɑhe	ɑhɛ	ɑxɛ	ɑxɛ	*ɑxɛ
87.	tongue	ɑnˈnɔdɑ	ɑnɛ : d	ɑnɛbɛd	ɑnɛbɛt	*ɑnnɛbɛt
88.	tooth	sɨ : ne	ʃin / ʃɨn	ʃin	ʃin	*sɨnn
89.	tree	jeʔe	jeʔɛ	eʔɛ	ɛt͡ʃˈɛ	*ɛt͡ʃˈɛ
90.	two	wʊˈʔɛ : ti	wirʔet / hurʔet	wirʔet	xʷet	*wirʔett
91.	warm	mɑʔoj-	mo : ʔ	mo : ʔ	mo : kʼ	*mʷakʼ
92.	water	ʔʊˈha	ihɛ / ixɛ	ixa	ixa	*ixa
93.	we	ɨnna	inɛ	ina	ina	*ɨnna
94.	wet	irˈramo	i : rɛ	zɨsu	zɨsu	*zɨsu
95.	what?	mʊn[8]	mɨr	mɨr	mɨr	*mɨr
96.	white	gɛd- e	ga : d	gʷa : d	gʷa : d	*gʷa : d
97.	who?	homun- e	ma : n	ma : n	mʷa : n	*mʷa : n
98.	woman	ɛ : (n)ʃta	miʃt / ẽ : ʃɛ (pl)	miʃt / it͡ʃa (pl)	miʃt / iʃta & iʃt͡ʃa (pl)	*miʃt
99.	you (m.pl.)	aˈhu : we	ahu :	axɨwa	axɨba / axwa	*axɨba

*The Mesmes text (appendix C) shows the more expected /bare/ form for 'say'. It is unclear why Bender's list shows the unexpected alternation /r:ɲ/.

The Mesmes data are from Bender (1971). The rest of the data are adapted from Leslau (1979). These data have been modified from the original lists. The phonetic transcription has been regularized using the

International Phonetic Alphabet, where possible. For the ease of maintaining geminate consonants across syllables, geminate consonants are written as doubles.

The PWG (Endegeny, Ennemor, and Gyeto) data contain a few uncommon symbols: Lelsau's [m̱], a spirantized bilabial nasal which is etically [m̥], is written as [m]; his [ḇ], a weakly articulated voiced bilabial stop, which is etically [ḇ], is written as [b]; and finally, Leslau's prepalatal velars[1] are written as [xʲ, gʲ]. These prepalatals are found in Ennemor and Gyeto.

The PWG reconstruction is my own, based upon the lexical and sound-change data presented in chapters 4 and 5. This reconstruction accounts only for the four forms (Mesmes, Endegeny, Ennemor, and Gyeto) in the above table, since it is assumed that each of these decended from a Proto-PWG mother.

Notes on the Mesmes Wordlist

The following numbers refer to the items in Bender's (1969) Mesmes wordlist. If a particular number is not listed below, the reader is to assume that the word is found throughout the CPWG Gurage languages. It may or may not be found in the other varieties of Mesqan, Muher, Gogot, Kistane, and Eastern Gurage.

The Hadiyya and Kambaata data are from Bender (1971). The Gurage data are from Leslau (1979).

2 the initial /h/ is found in Kistane and many of the non-OSE Ethio-Semitic languages (Leslau 1979, volume 3:47)[2]

4 unique to PWG with this meaning, except for /kɛrs/which is found in Soddo

---

[1] This is Leslau's terminology. It is assumed here that these are palatalized velars.

[2] It appears that Mesmes is more conservative, maintaining the initial laryngeal where other Gurage lects have lost it (#s 2,10,31,61,69 and 76 above). The initial laryngeals can be found in other Semitic languages like Hebrew and Arabic and often in some of the Ethio-Semitic languages such as Tigrinya, Argobba, Tigre and Gi'iz (Leslau 1979: volume 3). See table 4.16 and footnote 57 (4.2.4.1) for a brief discussion of the loss of the initial laryngeal and why it is not indicative of shared history.

Also cognate found: 'one who has big belly' in Mesqan, Gogot, Soddo[3]

5   unique to Mesmes; not found in Hadiyya or Kambaata

8   the meaning 'black person or object' is found only in Mesmes and Endegeny; the meaning 'black cow' is found throughout Gurage.

12 except in Mesmes, the /tks/ verb root is found throughout Gurage, as the second entry in Leslau (1979).

15 found throughout Gurage

16 unique to PWG and Soddo (with ejective /t'/ in Soddo) in Gurage; also found in the so-called East Gurage (see 1.4.2) languages; /tʃaɲa/ is found in Gyeto, while /mat'a/ must be seen as either very archaic or perhaps borrowed at the *Inor stage of development, thus resulting in reflexes for the three Inor forms, Endegeny, Ennemor, and Mesmes.

25 this word for 'fat' (nominal) is found only in Mesmes, Endegeny, Muher, Mesqan, Gogot, Soddo, and the East Gurage languages. That is, within CPWG Gurage, only the PWG speech forms Mesmes and Endegeny have it, according to Leslau (1979 volume 2:234).

29 possibly borrowed from Kambaata /tawɪ/ 'fly' (noun)

32 this word appears as the expected /wɛ : rɛ/ 'to go/to pass' in the Mesmes text (appendix C, lines 12 and 16); the origin of the Mesmes form here is unknown and may be related to the Amharic *hed-*.

33 unique to PWG (Ennemor, Endegeny, Mesmes); not in Gyeto or other Gurage languages

35 found throughout Gurage as 'hair of body'; the semantic shift is only in Mesmes.

---

[3] Ronny Meyer (personal communication: 2006) has kindly pointed out that this form occurs in other non-Ethiopian-Semitic languages, as well. It is my suggestion that while this form may have been borrowed into the Gurage family, this must have occurred at a time-depth early enough for the form to have undergone the expected changes in Mesmes.

39 unique to Mesmes; not found in Hadiyya or Kambaata

46 possibly borrowed from Hadiyya /afɛre/ 'liver'

47 found only in the East Gurage languages

50 unique to Mesmes; not found in Hadiyya or Kambaata (cf. 5)

53 unique to PWG: found in Endegeny with meaning 'mountain'—same as in Mesmes; also found as 'hill' in Ennemor and Gyeto.

57 possibly unique to PWG: (Ennemor, Endegeny, Mesmes); similar words /wɛrija/ and /we : rɛ/ found in Muher/Gogot and Zway, respectively.

58 all but the Mesmes form are related to the secondary entry in Leslau's dictionary: /miʃɛtɛ/ and /miʃɛdɛ/ in Cheha/Ezha/Muher and Endegeny, respectively; also related to Gogot and Soddo /miʃɛt/.

62 unclear relationship with other Gurage reflexes; typical correspondences would not lead to the expectation of the initial /g/ dropping in Ennemor and Endegeny; this may be a compound built on the same reflex found in East Gurage: /gɛnɛ/.

63 found throughout CWG and PWG (CPWG group); this reflex is found in Leslau, but not in Bender's list for Cheha.

65 unique to PWG: (Ennemor, Endegeny, Mesmes, and Gyeto)

66 found throughout Gurage (though not listed in Leslau 1979 for Ennemor) as 'bottom of thing'; the semantic shift is only in Mesmes.

67 unique to Mesmes; not found in Hadiyya or Kambaata

69 this Mesmes form for 'to see' may be borrowed from Amharic /aj : ɛ/; no other Gurage languages show this form.

73 the verb form in Mesmes is related to the nominal form for 'sleep' in the PWG languages; the maintenance of the pharyngeal as glottal stop is unique to PWG, but the reflex without the glottal can be

found throughout Gurage; it is not clear if the /n/ is present in the proto form or if the nasalization may be attributable to the glottal stop as discussed in section 4.2.4.1.

76   related to the form found in Endegeny; also found in Muher, Gogot, Soddo, and the East Gurage languages

77   unique to PWG: (Ennemor, Endegeny, Mesmes, and Gyeto)

80   possibly unique to PWG, not found in other CPWG group languages; possibly related to /imir/ in Gogot and /jimɨr/ in Soddo

81   possibly of Guragoid origin: reflex found in Mesqan /wak' : ɛ/, Gogot /wak' : ɛ-m/, and the East Gurage languages; also, the Mesmes word is quite similar to the Hadiyya and Kambaata words for 'swim'.

83   not found in CWG, but present in PWG, Muher, Mesqan, Soddo, and East Gurage.

84   unique to PWG (Ennemor, Endegeny, and Mesmes, but not found in Gyeto); the vowel in 'this' in the Mesmes text is a geminate /a/ (appendix C, line 7), as expected from the PWG examples.

89   this term most specifically refers to 'wood'; while Leslau includes the gloss 'tree' for the term, Ronny Meyer (personal communication, 2006) argues there is, apart from Amharic and North Ethiopic, no generic expression for 'tree' in Ethiopian-Semitic.

94   unique to PWG (Endegeny and Mesmes); not found elsewhere

96   found throughout Gurage

98   the word in Mesmes is the plural form for 'woman' elsewhere in Gurage; the coronal stop is not found in the example in the Mesmes text (appendix C, line 19).

Appendix B

Mesmes, Hadiyya, and Kambaata Comparison

MESMES, HADIYYA, AND KAMBAATA COMPARISON[1]

#	English	Mesmes	Hadiyya	Kambaata
1.	all	ɔtˈtɛmi	hunda	hora : nk
2.	ashes	hawɛnda	-butʃa	t'abaro
3.	bark (tree)	ha : nna	hoˈbara	omola
4.	belly	kɔssa	goˈdɛbo	gʷɔdɛ : ba
5.	big	k'ɔk'ɔ	lo : b	abba
6.	bird	ɔ : nfa	tʃ'i : ʔa	tʃ'i : ʔɛta
7.	bite (v)	ˈnakɔse	gɛʔme	gɛʔtmi̠
8.	black	gɔmbɔnna	he : ˈm-	gɛmˈbella
9.	blood	dɔ	t'i : ga	k'ɛ : gi
10.	bone	hãu̠wa	mik'e	miˈk'-
11.	breast	t'uwiye	anu : na	aˈnu : na
12.	burn (tr. v)	totosɔ	ʃokise	bussi
13.	claw	ʊnfura	t'uˈrɛ : nk'a	t'ulunga
14.	cloud	do : na	du : ba	go : ma
15.	cold	zi : z- ə	k'i : da	giˈda
16.	come	-mmaʔa	wa : re	wa : l(i)
17.	die	mɔtɔ-	lehe	reh
18.	dog	gi : ye	wʊʃ-	wɛˈʃ : -
19.	drink (v)	sɛˈt͡ʃɔ	age	ag : e

[1] The Hadiyya and Kambaata data are taken from Bender (1971).

Appendix B

20.	dry (adj)	dəˈro- e	goge	mo : la
21.	ear	ʊnˈzu : ra	mɛtʃʼe :	mɛtʃʼ-
22.	eat	baʔˈnɔ :	ite	i : t
23.	egg	kʼu : ra	kʼu : nkʼa	kʼuˈpʼ-
24.	eye	i̟ : n	ille	ɪlˈlita̱
25.	fat (n)	t͡ʃʼomma	diʔira	maʃe : la
26.	father	a : we	anna	anna
27.	fire	iˈsa : de	gi : ra	girɛta̱
28.	fish (n)	---	---	---
29.	fly (n)	ta : je	bi : mbeʔe̱	tawi̱
30.	foot	i̟gˈgi̟re	lokko	lokkata
31.	give	haˈmɔ-	ʔu : we	a : ss
32.	go	hɔˈrɔ : -	mɛre	i̟ro : kʼi
33.	good	moˈʔo	dɛna : m-	dɛˈna : -
34.	grass	saʔari	hitʼe :	hitʼi-
35.	hair (of head)	duˈgʊ : ra	odˈda :	mu : miya
36.	hand	idʒdʒa	anga	anˈg-
37.	head	gʊnnure	hoˈro : re	bokʼuta
38.	hear	sɔˈʔma	mɛˈtʃʼese	mɛtʃʼo : tʃ
39.	heart	nu : ba	wɛˈdɛno	wɔˈzɛna
40.	horn	kɔnna	bu : do	bu : ˈda
41.	I	hijˈja	ane	a : ni̱

42.	kill	ɔ : tɔrɔ	ʃi : he	ʃi :
43.	know	ha'ro : -	leʔe	dɛg(i)
44.	knee	gʊnno : da	gu-t'ub	gulubita
45.	leaf	ko'ʔora	bujja	bɔnta
46.	liver	fɔre	afɛre	a'fɛlita
47.	long	gʊd'dɔr-	k'e : 'raʔl	k'era : rʷa
48.	louse	k'u'wa : na	i'bi : ba	i'bi : -
49.	man	səwʲe	mɛn-	mɛn-
50.	many	k'ok'o	lobakata̰	ho : 'lama
51.	meat	bɔ'sɔra	ma : ra	ma : 'la
52.	moon	dən'naʔa	a'gɛna	a'gɛn-tʃu
53.	mountain	a : nja	du : na	du : na
54.	mouth	anfe	su : me	a'fo : ha
55.	name	ʃum	summa	suʔm
56.	neck	angɔda	ga : ndʒe	go : b-
57.	new	wɔj'jamo	ha : retʃ(o)	ha : roha
58.	night	haʷɔnʃɔde	hi : mo	anka'rija
59.	---	---	---	---
60.	nose	an'fʊnna	sɛne	sɛ'nuta
61.	one	ha : ti	ʃɛto	mɛto
62.	other	gən'namune	mull-	wɛ : lu
63.	rain (n)	di : je	t'e : na	t'e : 'na

Appendix B

64.	red	bi : ʃa	kɛˈʃa : r(a)	bi : ʃa
65.	road	mo : ja	go : go	wɔ : ˈkʼaha
66.	root	kʼine	nɪgga	tʼɛˈpʼa
67.	sand	tʼo : na	ʃeʃerą	ʃa : fa
68.	say	-beɲɔ : - *	jiˈhe	ji :
69.	see	-ha : ʲjɔ : -	mo : ʔe	tʼu : dį
70.	seed	zur(i)ji	wi : tʼo	zɛrɪtta
71.	sit	-t͡ʃɔna : -	aˈfu : re	afu : ʔl
72.	skin (human)	go : ga	o : mɛ : tʃo	go : ga
73.	sleep (v)	-wɔdɔ(ʔɔ)-	diˈri : re	usɛʔe
74.	small	ʊ : nse	ho : f-	kʼawa
75.	smoke (n)	tonna	wɪˈri : ra	wiˈle : lita
76.	snake	hawa : j	ha : mɛʃʃ-	wɛˈr-
77.	stand	-təʃəkkɔ-	ʔulle	u-rrį
78.	star	hõhõje	bolˈlanką	bɛze : -
79.	stone	oųna	kina	kino
80.	sun	ime :	e : ˈli : n-	arˈrɛ-u
81.	swim	-waʔa :	wa : tʃe	wa : tʃ
82.	tail	dʒuʔe	ʃerimo	ʃerįma
83.	thin	kʼɔt͡ʃt͡ʃʼina	witʃʼ	kʼɛtʃʼawa
84.	this	wʊ : -	kuki	kan-
85.	three	sɔ : sti	sɛso	sɛso

86.	you (sg)	ahe	ate	atį
87.	tongue	anˈnɔda	alˈlɛbo	arˈrɛbita
88.	tooth	sɨ : ne	ɪnkʼe	ɪnˈkʼutą
89.	tree	jeʔe	hakʼa	hakʼa
90.	two	wʊˈʔɛ : ti	lɛmu	lɛmo
91.	warm	maʔoj-	i : bˈbal-	i : ba
92.	water	ʔʊˈha	woʔo	wʊʔa
93.	we	ɨnna	ne : se	naˈʔɔ
94.	wet	irˈramo	a : ʃal	mu : tʼaʷa
95.	what?	mʊn¹⁰	maha	ma
96.	white	gəd- e	kʼɛˈdal-	wɔdʒʷa
97.	who?	homun- e	a : jje	aj
98.	woman	ɛ : (n)ʃta	mɛ : nt-	mɛ : nˈt-
99.	you (pl)	aˈhu : we	kʼiʔne	ʔatnɔʔ

*The Mesmes text (appendix C, line 7) shows the more expected /bare/ form for 'say'. It is unclear why Bender's list shows the unexpected alternation /r:ɲ/.

**In Bender's published list, /mʊnn : e/ is found, yet his unpublished notes suggest that the final /-ne/ is a copula.

These data have been modified from Bender's original lists (1971). The phonetic transcription has been regularized using the International Phonetic Alphabet. For the ease of maintaining geminate consonants across syllables, geminate consonants are written as doubles.

Appendix C

The Mesmes Text

1

iʃi bɛ-tɛʔeɲɲawʊd aβo-ɲ areʔ ɛ-wɔʔr
okay at-birth/childhood father-1SPO cow 3SM-guard.cattle

banɛ-d areʔ ɛ-wɔʔr banɛ-d
EXIST.PAST-MVM cow 3SM-guard.cattle EXIST.PAST-MVM
እሺ፡ ከተወለድኩብት አባቴ ከብት ያረባ ነበር (ከብት ያረባ ነበር)።
Okay, during (my) childhood, my father was taking care of cattle.

2

aβo-ɲ ti-kɛʃʃ-e areʔ ɛ-wɔʔr nɛbbɛr
father-1SPO when-send-1SObj cow 1S-guard.cattle EXIST.PAST

ba-bar-e bɛ-de : ŋginɛd-iɲa areʔ ɛ-wɔʔr nɛbbɛr
if-say-1SObj in-childhood-1SPO cow 1S-guard.cattle EXIST.PAST
አባቴ ሲልከኝ ከብት አረባ ነበር። ካለኝ በልጅነት ከብት አረባ ነበር።
When my father sent me, I took care of the cattle. If, during my childhood, he told me to, I guarded the cattle.

3

la : j-ɨggʊd afor ɛ-tʃʷɔd nɛbbɛr
then-after land 1S-farm EXIST.PAST
ከዚያ በኋላ መሬት አርስ ነበር።
After that, I was farming.

4

aβo-ɲ ɛ-kɛʃʃ-u wɛd ɛ-kkɛʃʃ nɛbbɛr adod-jome
father-1SPO REL.-sent-3MP place 1S-PASS.sent EXIST.PAST mother-1SPO

ɛ-kɛʃʃ-ɛtʃtʃ-e-dɨ ɛ-kkɛʃʃ nɛbbɛr bɛ-ha : wɛd
REL.-sent-3SF-1SOBJ-SFX 1S-PASS.sent EXIST.PAST after-that

tɛra : ʔ-ɛˈhu
grow-1S.MAIN.PAST
አባት የላኩኝ ቦታ እላክ ነበር። እናቴ የላከችኝ ቦታ እላክ ነበር። በኋላ አደግኩ።
I went to the place where my father sent me, and I went to where my mother sent me. After that, I grew up.

Appendix C 111

5

i-bi : d	bi-ho : no-i-w-ɛd	tɛ-bi : d-iɲa	konnt'om ik'a :
to-house	when-be-1S-SFX	from-house-1SPO	Hadiyya language

ziniki-ma	ti-ñ-žiñix	jɛsizi : ʔ
spoke-1P	when-1P-speak	after.that

ካገባሁ በኋላ (ካገባሁ በኋላ) ሐዲያ ቋንቋ እናገር ነበር። ከዚያም ስናገር፤

Beginning from the time when I married, we (my family) spoke Hadiyya. We were speaking after that...

6

ti-ñ-žiñix	jɛsizi : ʔ	waʔar-hʷ-'i :	zɛʔʔn-ɛ'hu
when-1P-speak	after.that	raised.cattle-1S-CONV	sowed-1S.CONV

tʃʷɔd-ɛ'hu	k'ɛbbɛr-'hu	ha : -hɛ	ø-anikk ba
plowed-1S.CONV	planted-1S.CONV	that-like	1S-do EXIST.PAST

ከዚያም ስናገር አርቢ ዘርቼ አርሼ ተክዬ፤ እንዳ አደርግ ነበር።

After that, I shepherded cattle, having sowed, plowed, and planted. That's what I was doing.

7

bɛ-ha : da	wa : da de : ŋga-ɲo	gɛ : ɾɛd a-gɛʔpa-'hu
after-that that	children-1SPO	girl CAUSE-marry-1S.CONV

k'o't'ok'o't'o	barɛ-'hu	ha : -hɛ	a-ra : ʔ-ɛhu
arrange.in.orderly.manner	say-1S.CONV	that-like	CAUSE-grow-1S

ከዚያ በኋላ ለልጆቼ ልጃገረድ ድሬያቸው ቦታ ቦታ አስይዤ እንዳ አሳደኩአቸው።

After that, I arranged marriages for my sons. Having settled them, arranging them in various places, I raised them.

8

ha : -n	de : ŋga-ɲa	waʔaka	tɛra : ʔ-ɛ	hudua
that-be	children-1SPO	now	grow-3MS	they

ha : -m-n-ua
that-MAIN.PAST-be-3MP

እንደዚያ ልጆቼ አሁን አድገው እነሱም እንዳ ናቸው።

Now, my children have grown; and (now), they are living like that (raising their own kids).

9

ba-ha : -ɨggʊd aβo-ɲo-gat   t-awaʔonɛd   sojgiʔ
after-then-after father-1SPO-time with-awak'inet (religious title) time

wɨr   i : m   ba   wi   i : m ba
ox   3M.give EXIST.PAST   honey 3M.give EXIST.PAST
ከዚያ በኋላ አባቴ በአዋቅነት ጊዜ (መንፈሳዊ መሪ በነበረ ጊዜ) በሬ ይሰጡ ነበር ማር ይሰጡ ነበር።
After that, (they) were giving oxen and honey to my father, during his time as Awak'in (a ritual leader in the bʷɛʒɛ cult).

10

agɛɲɛrʊ   aɲ-ɛ-ʔeɲɲɛ   hʊd   ɛ-ʔeɲɲ-i
poor   NEG-REL-give.birth   he   3M-give.birth-PURPOSIVE

maʔ-'ɛ   ɛ-sɔʔɨr   nɛbbɛr
come-3MS.CONV   3M-begged   EXIST.PAST
የተቸገረ ያልወለደ ለመወልድ መጥቶ ይለምን ነበር
The poor (and) those who lacked children, in order to give birth, came and were begging.

11

a-ti-i-sɛʔr-i   wɨr ø-agaʔ   nɛbbɛr   iw
after.that-when-3-beg-PURPOSIVE ox 3M-CAUSE.enter EXIST.PAST honey

ø-agaʔ   nɛbbɛr   hado   da : r-un-'tɛ
3M-CAUSE.enter   EXIST.PAST   after.that bless-3MPL-SFX.MAIN.PAST
ከዚያም ሊለምን በሬ ያመጣ ማር ያመጣ ነበር። ከዚያ ይመርቁዋቸው ነበር።
In order to beg, they were bringing in oxen and honey. After that, he blessed them.

12

ha : -ʔamɨ-sojʔ   ti-i-da : r-uwɛ-tu   aɲ-ɛ-ʔeɲɲɛ
that-be-time   when-3M-blessed-3MPL-SFX   NEG-REL-give.birth

hʊd wɛ : r-'ɛ   ɛ-ʔeɲɲɛ   ba
he went-3MS.CONV   3M-give.birth   EXIST.PAST
በዚያን ጊዜ ሲመረቁ ያልወለደው ሄዶ ይወልድ ነበር።
At that time, once they were blessed, those who were not giving birth went

Appendix C

and were giving birth.

13

ize : gɛ	hʊd ɛ-ʔʊf	ban	arɛʔ	aggɛl-ˈɛ
poor	the 3M-be.sated	EXIST.PAST	cattle	raised.cattle-3MS.CONV

k' ɛbbɛr-ˈɛ	ha : -hɛ	ɛ-ʔʊf	banɛ-d
plant-3MS.CONV	that-like	3M-be.sated	EXIST.PAST-MVM

የደኸየው· ይጠግብ ነበር። ከብት ያረባ፥ የተከለ እንደዚያ ይጠግብ ነበር።

The poor were satisfied. Having raised cattle and planted (crops, probably inset—the false banana tree, a Gurage staple), they were satisfied (This is to be understood to be a result of the blessing.)

14

bɛ-ha : -ʔiggʊd	aβo-ɲ	t-i-mowɛd	hukko
after-then-after	father-1SPO	when-3MS-died	like.this

ha : mmɛdɛ	t-uiʔio-i	gebbɛr-ˈhu
like.this/that	?	pay.taxes-1S.CONV

ከዚያ በኋላ አባቴ ሲሞት እንደ (?) ገብሬ

Later, after my father died, I paid taxes,

15

tʃʷɔd-ɛˈhu	waʔar-ɛˈhu	ha : -hɛ	hija	ɛ-hɛnɛr
plowed-1S.CONV	guard.cattle-1S.CONV	that-like	I	1S-be

አርሼ (ከብት) እያረባሁ· እንደዚያ እኖራለሁ።

plowed, and took care of the cattle; I lived like that.

16

ba-ha : da wa : da waʔaka	ɛ-wɛ : r-ɛ	mɛngist	ti-n-gebbɛr
after-that that now	REL-pass-3M	government	when-1P-pay.taxes

ti-n-t-akkid	ti-n-t'ɛd	ha : -hɛ	ɛ-hɛnɛr
when-1P-PASS-be.bound	when-1P-be.released	that-like	1S-be

ሁሉም ነገር ካለፈ በኋላ አሁን ለመንግሥት ስንገብር ስንታሠር ስንፈታ፥ እንደዛ ኖርኩ።

After all that, now, we are paying taxes to the various governments, we being bound, we being released...I lived like that.

17

waʔaka	mɨhɛmɨ?	waʔaka-hɛ	tʃʷɔd-ɛh-ˈi :
now	likewise	now-like	plow-1S-PURPOSIVE.CONV

waʔar-ɛhʷ-ˈi :	ha : -hɛ	geb : ɨrɨ-nn-ɨtɛ
guard.cattle-1S-PURPOSIVE.CONV	that-like	farming-be.3M-SFX

አሁን እንደዚያ ነው። አሁን እንደዚያ አርሼ አግጄ እንደዚያ በግብርና

Now, as well, farming is in the same manner: plowing and taking care of cattle.

18

ha : -hɛ	tʃɨmtʃud	ha : -hɛ	ɲɛʔɛ-ˈhu	an : ɛ-hu
that-like	field	that-like	spend.night-1S.CONV	EXIST-1S

እንደዚያ እያረስኩ ውዬ እያደርኩ እኖራለሁ።

This is how I've lived, spending my days in the field and my nights at home.

19

bɛ-ha : -ʔɨggud	(i)duro	gaʔat	zɛm	aβo-ɲa
after-then-after	formerly	dawn	period.of.time	father-1SPO

b-awnst	e : ʃi	(i)ʔeɲɲ-ˈɛ
by-five	women	give.birth-3MS.MAIN.PAST

ከዚያ በኋላ ድሮ ጧት አባቴ ካምስት ሴቶች ወለደዋል

Back in the beginning, my father begot children by five women.

20

b-awnst	ʔeɲɲ-uwɛ-tu	huʔja	wɛdkɛ
by-five	give.birth-3MPL-SFX	twenty	?

de : ŋga	ha : -hɛ	nor-ɛ
children	that-like	lived-3MS

ከአምስት ሴቶች ሃያ ልጆች ወልዶ ነበር። እንደዚያ ኖረ።

By five women, he begot twenty children. He lived like that.

Appendix D

Notes on the Analysis of the Mesmes Text

The text is broken up into twenty meaningful units, most of which are sentences or clusters of clauses. The numbers in the notes below correspond to these meaningful units. Not every word is discussed; rather the focus in these notes is on selected features (syntactic, morphological, lexical, and phonological) of the Mesmes text and their relationship to other Gurage lects as described in Hetzron 1977 and Leslau 1979 and 1992.

If a word or structure is found in multiple places in the text, the discussion of the feature is typically handled in the notes on the line of the feature's first occurrence.

Line 1:

> According to Leslau (1979), the word for 'birth' is /t'inwɛt/ with the /n/ geminate in Cheha. Leslau does not include the nominal forms in Ennemor or Endegeny for this word. But the /t→d/ found in Mesmes is indeed expected, as seen elsewhere in the text and the wordlist.
>
> Hetzron writes that /bɛ-/ means 'in' and 'from' (1977:243) while with the high central vowel, it means 'when' in Ennemor. It is also possible, though not in this context, for /bɛ-/ to refer to the conditional 'if' (Hetzron 1977:241).
>
> Leslau's Gurage dictionary provides the following for the verb 'to guard cattle': Cheha /ɛre warɛ-m/, Ezha /ɛre warɛ-m/, Ennemor /areʔ waʔarɛ/, Endegeny /areʔ waʔarɛ/, and Gyeto /araj waʔarɛ/. The vowel in Mesmes appears to have backed in the imperfect. Yet, in later examples (lines 6, 15, 17), in the perfect, the vowel is indeed /a/. As mentioned in 4.2.4.3, there is a tendency for vowels to undergo a degree of neutralization in closed syllables, with /ɛ/, /o/ → /ɔ/ and /ɨ/, /u/ → /ʊ/, respectively (see section 4.2.4.3.). There is some contrast (suspicious, as it is) between /o/ and /ɔ/. That is, [ʊ, ɔ] do appear to be phonemes in Mesmes. This is quite possibly a feature which has arisen from contact with Hadiyya and Kambaata (Highland East Cushitic).

Line 2:

> In contrast to the PWG existential /banɛd/ in line 1, here the Amharic existential /nɛbbɛr/ occurs. While this form is present in

Appendix D 117

Soddo/Kistane, there is no reason to assume this has been inherited by a Peripheral West lect. There is a Peripheral West cognate /nɛppɛrɛ/ 'to live' which is related to the Amharic existential.

The temporal morpheme /t-/ found throughout Hetzron's Ennemor texts (1977:243, line 5) is identical in Mesmes, but in Mesmes it is often voiced in the most sonorant environments. Since the voicing of the /t-/ is predictable, it is not shown in the transcription. Voicing occurs in lines 2 and 14.

The Gurage words for 'childhood' are: Cheha /tɨknɛt/, Ezha /tɨknnɛt/, Ennemor /de : ngʲinɛd/, Endegeny /de : ngɨnɛd/, and Gyeto /de : ngʲinɛt/ (Leslau 1979). The Mesmes example shows relationship with Endegeny through the loss of the prepalatal /gʲ/ (as seen in Ennemor and Gyeto) as well as the two examples of /t→d/ voicing.

The /-e/ 1S object agreement (complement suffix) is the same as found in Ennemor (Hetzron 1977:238).

Line 3:

The verb stem for 'farm' is: Cheha/Ezha /tʃotɛ/, Ennemor/Endegeny /tʃo : dɛ/, and Gyeto /tʃo : tɛ/. The postposition /-ɨggʊd/ is also found in Leslau's dictionary as 'after'. Again, the existential here is borrowed from Amharic.

Line 4:

The verb stem /kɛʃʃɛ/ is unique to PWG (Peripheral West Gurage), found only in Mesmes, Ennemor, and Endegeny. Gyeto and Cheha and some West Gurage languages have /na:xɛ/ for 'send' (Leslau 1979).

The t→ d correspondence is seen in 'mother' where Cheha and other Sebat Bet Gurage have /t/ and PWG exhibits /d/.

The same /ɛ-/ marker for the relative clause is found in Mesmes as in Hetzron's texts. However, the suffix /-dɨ/ is unexpected here. The so-called k/t/d suffixes (Hetzron 1977:92) are found throughout PWG. Their distribution is inherited from the ancient main verb markers (1977:93). While the -d suffix is expected after a short vowel or a consonant which is part of a suffix (1977:92), the -k after a radical, the -t after a geminate vowel or diphthong, the -d suffix is not expected on the past relative. In Ennemor, it is found on the main negative verbs and the relative nonpast—among other forms. Ronny Meyer has suggested that this may be a reflex of the locative suffix, /-et/, /-ət/, or /-t/ in Wolane or Muher (personal communication, 2006).

As for the passive constructions, Hetzron writes: "The element /tɛ-/ (-t- after prefixes often assimilated to the next consonant), attached to type A or type B forms constitutes the passive-reflexive…" (1977:72) In line 4, the prefix is dropped due to the presence of subject agreement marking in the imperfect form. As a result, the first radical is geminated, as Hetzron describes.

With regard to the plural agreement morphology, it must be mentioned that Hetzron notes the phenomenon of labial harmony, with left-spreading labialization attaching as off-glides to consonant radicals in Endegeny verbs containing a suffix with /u/ (1977:81). Leslau notes that /-um/ is the 3MPL agreement marker for the perfect form in Endegeny (1992:467). There is no evidence of this sort of labial harmony affecting consonants to the left in Mesmes. There is, however, some labial impact on vowels, as noted below in the note for line 5.

The main verb in line 4 is marked with the final stressed vowel, what Hetzron terms the main past marker. Originally, this was the suffix /-m/ (related to the /-m/ enclitic). Just as has occurred with the loss of the /-m/ converb marker (see the note on line 6), the stress, which was placed on the final closed syllable, is maintained despite the loss of the final consonant (Hetzron 1977:42–43). Of special note here is the fact that these processes lead to a loss of contrast between main verbs in the perfect and subordinate verbs which are marked as converbs. That is, main verbs (in the perfect) and subordinate verbs appear identical phonetically. Hetzron, in his grammatical glosses, does note the distinction, using *C* for the stressed final vowels that are converb markers and *M* for the stressed final vowels that are marking the main past or the /-m/ enclitic (see Hetzron 1977:236, text 19, line 6 for an example of both forms on one line). Not every

Appendix D

main verb in the perfect in the Mesmes text is marked with this final stressed vowel. Main verbs in the perfect which are not marked as main past: lines 5 /zinɨki-ma/ 'spoke-1P', 7 /a-ra : ʔ-ɛhu/ 'CAUSE-grow-1S', and 18 /an : ɛ-hu/ 'EXIST-1S'.

Main verbs in the perfect which are marked as main past: lines 4 / tɛra : ʔ-ɛ'hu/ 'grow-1S.MAIN.PAST', 11 /da : r-un-'tɛ/ 'blessed-3MP-SFX.MAIN.PAST', and 19 /(ɨ)ʔeɲɲ-'ɛ/ 'give.birth-3MS.MAIN.PAST'.

Since it appears that all the so-called Gunnän Gurage languages (Soddo/Kistane, Gogot/Dobi, Muher, Mesqan, CWG lects, and PWG lects) have the m-converb form, and that the m-converb construction includes the perfect + -m as well as other forms of the verb, it is most likely that this /-m/ as a converb marker was the earlier form and that in the so-called 3G (CPWG Gurage—which is Central West and Peripheral West Gurage) languages the /-m/ ending was generalized to become the marker for the main past verbs (in the perfect + -m) form. It is unclear whether the /-m/ enclitic or the /-m/ converb is the older form, though it certainly seems likely that they are related. It must be admitted, however, that the /-m/ enclitic, as a discourse function word, is also found in Amharic outside of Outer South Ethiopic.

Line 5:

The first phrase in line 5 is an idiomatic expression which is also found in Hetzron's Ennemor text (1977:244, line 24): /ɛ-bi : d-hunoa hõːr-mʷ-ta/. Hetzron parses this Ennemor example as follows: to-house-their were-CONV-ta. According to Hetzron, Polotsky says the /-ta/ element comes from 'when-there+is' /t-anɛ/. Hetzron says its function is to "break up the monotony of converbs and indicate a relative hierarchy of the breaks between them" (1977:244). The high central vowel (stressed) before the -ta element may be omitted in PWG (1977:98). I assume that the -d in the Mesmes ending is a reflex of this -ta and that the -Vw is probably the converbial marker in the Mesmes example. Hetzron does note the phonological correspondence of /mʷ/ becoming /w/ in Endegeny (1977:50).

The verb /hoːno/ is the copula. This form is clearly related to Ennemor: /xẽrɛ/ and Endegeny /hɛ : nɛ/ (Leslau 1979). Presumably, the vowels in the Mesmes copula have undergone backing, akin to what Leslau found in perfect verb forms in Endegeny (1992:467). In this case, however, the process is a result of the /w/ not a /u/.

According to Leslau, /k'ar/ is the word for 'language' in Ennemor (1979). The initial vowel is likely epenthetic in Mesmes. The final /r/ consonant has been lost with compensatory gemination of the vowel as the result.

The verb 'to speak' is cognate with other PWG languages. There appears to be a word-final weakening process in Mesmes where /k→ x/. In the Ennemor form for 'speak' the /k/ is maintained and not weakened word-finally (Leslau 1992). I have not been able to determine the meaning of the word /jɛsizi : ʔ/ in the Mesmes text. It is not found in Leslau's data and was unknown to my Ennemor contacts. The meaning is not determinable from the Mesmes speaker's own translation of his text, which was primarily on the sentence level and does not include every word or morpheme.

Line 6:

The nature of the /i/ vowel suffix on the verb /waʔar-hʷ-'i : / 'to raise cattle' is unclear. Hetzron notes (1977:89) that /-i/ is one of the main verb markers in Gogot (Dobi), attaching to the perfect main verb with no complement suffixes, where the subject is 1SG. Polotsky, according to Hetzron, traces the /-i/ back to /-u/ which followed short vowels and consonants (while the -n/-tt was following original long vowels). This /-i/ is formed through dissimilation with the labial of /kʷ/ and /hʷ/. There is the possibility, though quite unlikely in my opinion, that the suffix may be postpositional (Hetzron 1977:55), though the meaning of 'toward' does not seem to fit any applicative that would be expected in the context of this verb, such as benefactive might. Also, there is the common PWG /-i/ ending which marks the purposive (Hetzron 1977:99). The purposive is found in the Mesmes text in lines 10, 11, and 17. It is unclear if the context in line 6 could warrant the use of the purposive.

There appear to be four converbial constructions in line 6. The stressing of the final vowel on the verbs, 'sow', 'plow', and 'plant' marks the m-converb (Hetzron 1977:94). Converbs are used throughout Ethio-Semitic languages and many OV-type languages, to join multiple clauses or verbs through a chaining mechanism where only the final verb is fully inflected.

I assume the stressing of the final vowel in PWG to be the result of a compensatory process. Outside of PWG, in Gurage, converbs are marked with a verb in the perfect form, followed by an /-m/. It is my argument that the /-m/ is lost in PWG and the final vowel is then lengthened. Hetzron does not discuss this process as compensatory, but simply notes the 'stressed' status of the final vowels and the loss of the /-m/. Since duration is often an important component of stress, it is quite possible that Hetzron's 'stress' (1977:94) is underlying a long vowel, which is filling two timing units, compensating for the loss of the /-m/.

An interesting find is that the Mesmes word for 'to plant' does not exhibit the same merger of glottalized sounds to the glottal stop that is evidenced in PWG: /ʔɛpɛrɛ/ in Ennemor and /ʔɛppɛrɛ/ in Endegeny (Leslau 1979). This word in Mesmes also fails to show the expected (and attested elsewhere in the data—line 7, 'to marry') devoicing of the geminate second radical of the verb root, common in PWG but not elsewhere in Gurage. As a result of Mesmes' lack of participation in these expected innovations, it seems likely that this word is borrowed from another Gurage language. Words inherited through normal transmission would be expected to show these innovations.

I have been unable to find other attestations of the verb 'to do' /anɨkk/ outside of the Mesmes text. My Ennemor contacts immediately recognized the word to mean 'do', yet it is not found in Hetzron's texts or in Leslau's dictionary. The word was originally translated by the Mesmes speaker (through a Hadiyya-Amharic bilingual) as 'managing'. The root for 'do' in PWG is /epɛ/ in Ennemor and /eppɛ/ in Endegeny (Leslau 1979).

It appears that the 1S agreement prefix on the verb 'to do' for this imperfect form is lost due to the presence of the initial /a/. This same phenomenon may be observed on the verb 'to enter' in line 11, though in the latter case, the prefix is the 3S—identical in phonological form to the 1S, due to the leveling described in section 3.6.1.

The existential in Gurage is typically a form related to /banɛ/ (Hetzron 1977), as in line 1. Hetzron adds, "Outside of Soddo, an invariable ba may also be used, especially when it acts as an auxiliary." (1977:106). This reduced form, functioning as an auxiliary, is found in lines 6, 9, and 12.

Line 7:

Leslau's dictionary does not show this word for 'child' or 'children'. A form of it is listed for 'childhood' (see notes on line 1). Hetzron does, however, show it in his texts (1977:244, line 25), where /de : ngʲa/ is glossed as 'children'. My Ennemor contacts have suggested that /dengɛ/ is the singular while /dengo/ is the plural.

The verb stem for 'to marry', as in other Ethio-Semitic languages, is formed from the verb 'to enter' —/gɛppaʔa/ in Endegeny (Leslau 1979). The following list provides Leslau's data on 'to marry' in Western Gurage: Cheha /(a)gɛpa-m/, Ezha /(a)gɛbba-m/, Ennemor /(a)gɛpa/, Endegeny /(a)gɛppaʔa/, and Gyeto /(a)gɛpa/. The Mesmes example /a-gɛʔpa/ shows the maintenance of the pharyngeal in the form of the glottal stop, as does Endegeny. Mesmes, however, has undergone metathesis, reversing the order of the stop and glottal. This is a common process, often shared by both Endegeny and Mesmes (see 4.2.4.4). The last vowel of this verb is stressed, marking it as a converb.

As in Amharic, Gurage has verb complexes which employ the use of the verb 'to say' /barɛ/. Throughout Gurage, according to Leslau (1979), the verb /k'ut'k'ut'barɛ/ is found, meaning something along the lines of 'to sit properly, in an arranged fashion'. The last vowel of this verb 'say' is stressed, indicating its marking as a converb.

The /a-/ prefix on the final verb is a valence increaser, essentially the causative marker, seen also on the verb 'to marry'. For a clear comparison between this causative 'to grow' and the intransitive, see the last word in line 4.

Appendix D

Line 8:

The Gurage languages exhibit a bound copula. The following chart provides a few of the examples from Ennemor (Hetzron 1977:106):

-nhʷ-	1SG
-nɨra-	1PL
-n-	3MSG
-noa-	3MPL

Hetzron claims that the shape of the Ennemor bound copula is indicative of PWG in general. Syntactically, the copula tends to be the second-to-the-last element in the word in PWG; it is syntactically free in Muher, and word final elsewhere (1977:106).

Hetzron writes that when the last word has any suffix, the copula does attach before that suffix (as in /hɑ : -m-n-uɑ/ here), but in the case where the sentence-final word has no suffix, the copula will be the final element.

The Mesmes word 'now' /wɑʔɑkɑ/ is clearly cognate with PWG: Cheha /ɛxʷɑ/, Ezha /ɛxʷɑ/, Ennemor /wɑʔɑkɑ/, Endegeny /wɑʔɑkkɛ/, and Gyeto /ɛxʷɑ/ (Leslau 1979). This word appears to be unique to Ennemor, Endegeny, and Mesmes.

There is an interesting phenomenon in the 3MPL pronoun /hudua/. According to Leslau, the Endegeny 3MS and 3MPL are /hudɛ/ and /huno:/, respectively (1979). In Ennemor the form for 3M and 3MPL are /xutɛ/ and /hunoa/. It should be mentioned that, as it does in Mesmes, the 3M pronoun /huda/ (Hetzron 1977:58) also serves as the definite article in Ennemor (243, line 2). Lines 10, 12, and 13 of the Mesmes text show the Mesmes form for 3M is /hʊd/. An interesting problem is why does Mesmes not have a nasal for the second consonant in the 3MPL form. Mesmes may have reanalyzed its pronominal paradigm, interpreting the final vowel(s) on the pronouns as agreement markers. It must be pointed out that the ending for the 3M /-ɛ/ (lost in the connected speech of the text, but evident in the wordlist) is homophonous with the 3M subject agreement suffix found on perfect verbs. Also, the /-ua/ on the Mesmes 3MPL pronoun is the same as the 3MPL subject agreement ending on verbs in the perfect form. It could be that the /hʊd/ has come to mean 3M and the final vowels denote number accordingly. This could account for the loss of the nasal.

Line 9:

The initial transition word is certainly related to the Endegeny complex of preposition and postposition meaning 'after': /bɛ__e : ggɛd/ (Leslau 1979). The transition word in Endegeny, however, does not employ the preposition-postposition complex; it requires the time word /gidɑ : d/ as in /bɛ-hɑ gidɑ : d/: literally, 'at-that time'. The Mesmes example shows the use of the pre-postposition as a transition mechanism. It must be recalled that multifunctionality among discourse markers is the norm.

The prepositional /t-/, marking accompaniment on /t-ɑwɑʔonɛd/, is found in Hetzron's Ennemor texts as well (1977:235, line 1). The root here is related to /wakʼ/ 'god of war'. One of my Ennemor contacts reports that the speaker was serving as the /ɑwɑʔin/ or /ɑwɑʔined/. This term is likely related to the ritual dignitary of Wakʼ (the War God)'s title, as reported by Shack and Habte /ɑbɛkʼʲɛ/ (1974). They write:

> Religious dignitaries who represented the national deities, Wak, Bwaza and Damwamwit, could alone collect tribute from all Gurage directly, without regard for their clan and tribal affiliations, and also indirectly through their ritual agents who were headquartered in every clan of every tribe. (1974:19)

Shack and Habte also report that the Maga ('ritual agents' of the Thunder-God /bwɛʒɛ/'s representative /gwetɑkwɨjɛ/) are given the skin of every sacrificed animal (see Shack and Habte 1974:29, footnote 15). The Maga are also given honey, for ceremonial extinguishing of fires caused by lightning (see page 33, footnote 17). It may be that the gifts given in the Mesmes text, oxen and honey, are in some way related to this practice. One of my Ennemor contacts disagreed with Shack and Habte, saying that Wakʼ (the War God's name in Shack and Habte 1974) is actually in the service of the Thunder God, /bwɛʒɛ/, who is supreme. Thus, he concluded that Mesmes speaker's father, in the text, was in the service of /bwɛʒɛ/. To further complicate the matter, it must be mentioned that Leslau's Endegeny

Appendix D

dictionary gives /ɛwaʔ/ as the term for 'a person possessed by a spirit' (1979:160, vol. 1). Whatever the case with the Mesmes term, the fact remains that the speaker's father was an important religious figure who was given gifts and who offered blessings to those who came to him.

In the word /i : m/ 'give', the spirantized (weakly articulated) nasal in medial position is unique to PWG in this position: Cheha /abɛ-m/, Ezha /abɛ-m/, Ennemor [am̞ɛ̃], Endegeny [am̞ɛ̃], Gyeto [am̞ɛ̃] or [ab̞ɛ]¹ (Leslau 1979). Hetzron, in his Ennemor text number 20 (line 9), provides two forms for the verb 'give': /jī : m/ and [am̞ɛ̃] (1977:238). It is the first of the two forms that appears to be closely related to the Mesmes verb. This form for 'give' is not found in Hetzron's Gyeto texts; it is unique to Ennemor and Mesmes and thus, in my opinion, probably present in Endegeny as well. Ronny Meyer reports that the vowel changes /aa/ > /ee/ and /aa/ > /ii/ may be found in non-perfective conjugations of 'give' in Muher, Wolane and Zay (personal communication, 2006). Thus, it may be that this vocalic change is present in Mesmes, as well.

On the reduced auxiliary existential, see notes on line 6.

The Mesmes word for 'ox' /wɨr/ may be a reduction of the PWG example of the standard Gurage reflex, sharing the /w/: Cheha /bora/, Ezha /bora/, Ennemor /bawira/, Endegeny /bawrɛ/, Gyeto /bawra/ (Leslau 1979). This dropping may be due to contact with Hadiyya, in which final vowels are dropped in connected speech (Cf. chapter 5 on the addition of vowels under influence from Hadiyya.) The initial /ba/ has dropped as well in Mesmes, but the word is clearly recognizable to Ennemor speakers.

According to Leslau, 'honey' is /wɨjɛ/ in Cheha, Ennemor, Endegeny, Gyeto, Muher, Mesqan, and Gogot. The palatal is geminate in Ezha (1979:314). It may be that the environment of the word in the Mesmes text has masked this form as a simple /wi/.

I have been unable to determine the meaning of /sojgiʔ/ beyond doubt. It is not found in Leslau's dictionaries and no translation of the Mesmes text, by either the Mesmes speaker himself or two Ennemor speakers, provides clear indication of the meaning.

---

[1] The diacritic under the m and b ([m̞] and [b̞]) represents weak articulation.

Line 10:

The origin of /agɛɲɛru/ 'poor' is unclear. This word could be related to Leslau's 'be poor': Cheha /ɛdʒ at'ɛrɛ/, Ezha /ɛdʒ att'ɛrɛ/, Ennemor /ɛdʒ aʔɛrɛ/, Endegeny /ɛdʒ eʔɛrɛ/, Gyeto /ɛdʒ at'ɛrɛ/ (1979). The nasal in Mesmes could be due to rhinoglottophilia, as a result of the debuccalized ejective (as observed in table 4.17).

Leslau shows the negative for Endegeny verbs in the perfect to be /an- -dɛ/ (1992:468). This /an-/ is evidenced in the Mesmes negative relative. It is unclear if the palatal nature of the nasal in Mesmes is due to a sort of palatal harmony (akin to labialization harmony found in Endegeny and mentioned in 4.2.4.3). The only examples of this negative morpheme in Mesmes are on the verb 'to give birth', which contains a palatal nasal of its own (lines 10 and 12). Of interest here is the main verb marker /-d/, which is present on the relative perfect form in line 4 but absent in this negative relative perfect in 10. It is unclear why this is lost on the negative.

The verb 'to give birth' in Ennemor and Endegeny is /ʔeɲɲɛ/ and /tʃ'ɛnɛ/ elsewhere in Western Gurage. The Mesmes example certainly shows the same merger where glottalized sounds (ejectives) lose their place features through debuccalization.

See the note on line 8 for discussion surrounding the 3M pronoun/definite article. There is an /-i/ on the verb 'to give birth', marking purposive (Hetzron 1977:99). See note on line 6 for brief discussion. Etically (and thus not shown in the text transcription), the stem-internal vowel and the agreement prefix agree in height with this purposive suffix, raising the 3M /ɛ-/ to /i-/; this is not completely unlike the harmony Leslau noted in Endegeny: "In the plural, 3rd masculine, the vowels of the 1st and 3rd radicals change into o, undoubtedly under the influence of the ending -um" (1992:467).

The verb /maʔ-'ɛ/ 'to come' (also exhibiting the glottalized consonant merger—/t/ → /ʔ/ in PWG) is marked as a converb with slight stress on the final vowel. This construction is what Hetzron calls the durative habitual past (1977:96). In this case, the clauses can be literally translated 'came and were begging'. Converbs are also discussed in notes on lines 6, 7, 12, 13, 14, 15, 17, and 18).

Appendix D

The root for 'beg', /sɔʔɨr/, is unique to the Ennemor and Endegeny subgroup, according to Leslau's dictionary: /saʔarɛ/ 'beg' in PWG and /tʃɛk ' ʷɛsɛ/ elsewhere in Gurage.

Line 11:

I have been unable to determine the meaning of the initial /a-/. It may be a discourse marker. The vowel in the verb 'to beg' is fronted in the imperfect form here. This is quite different from what is found in line 10, also in the imperfect. This may be due to the [-back] status of the purposive suffix or possibly the prefix.

There is an unexpected vowel shape for 'when' /ti-/ and 3M marker. Why is the vowel the high front /i/? Hetzron notes that 3M imperfect prefix in PWG is /jɨ-/ or /j-/ while 3M jussive is /ɛ-/ without the glide (1977:80). Leslau notes the Endegeny 3M imperfect prefix is /ɨ-/ (the 1SG has also become /ɨ-/, according to Leslau [p.468]) while the 3M jussive is /ɛ-/. The important thing to note here is that in Endegeny (and in Mesmes) there does not appear to be a palatal glide in the 3M prefix, yet, after the temporal marker /t-/ the vowel is often raised to /i-/ just as would be expected if the glide had remained. In fact, in Ennemor, after the /t-/ temporal, the vowel for 3M is always /i/ (Hetzron 1977:101). Hetzron notes: "In general, ɨ is realized as [i] in contact with y and [u] in contact with w" (1977:141). It is unclear if the /j/ is present but not allowed to surface word initially. It is unlikely, but possible that when the /t-/ temporal attaches, the /j/ is then able to raise the vowels; otherwise it is simply dropped in the basic imperfect where no other prefix is needed. It may be that the remnant of the /j/ is only maintained in these instances where the /i/ surfaces as a result of morphophonological processes. Elsewhere in Mesmes, the /j/ is allowed word initially, though it is somewhat rare. Out of the ninety-nine words in Bender's list only 'tree' begins with a palatal—identical to the form found in Endegeny (the other Gurage forms do not have the palatal); see appendix A, item 89.

As mentioned in the note for line 7, the root for 'enter' in Gurage is Cheha /gɛpa-m/, Ezha /gɛbba-m/, Ennemor /gɛpa/, Endegeny /gɛppaʔa/, and Gyeto /gɛpa/ (Leslau 1979). It appears that Mesmes has metathesized the glottal and then dropped the rest: /agaʔpa/ to /agaʔ/. The metathesis is certainly expected. It could also be that the /p/ is maintained, but not heard in the imperfect form since hearing a /ʔp/ word finally would be quite difficult. Also, the 3M marker /ɛ-/ is dropped, as expected, when the root begins with a vowel.

The Mesmes word /hado/ is not found in the other Gurage literature. It was recognizable to my Ennemor contacts as meaning 'after that' and clearly the construction contains /ha-/ which is most probably related to 'that'.

The root for the verb 'to bless' is /dɑ : rɛ/ throughout Gurage. The geminate vowel, however, is unique to PWG, seen only in Leslau's data for Ennemor, Endegeny, and Gyeto (1979). Leslau also shows /-um/ as the 3MPL ending in Endegeny (1992:467). In the Mesmes text, the plural form is used to indicate politeness. This main verb is marked as main past by the final stressed vowel (see note on line 4).

Line 12:

Again, as in line 8, the bound copula is the second-to-the-last element in the word (/hɑ : -ʔamɨ-sojʔ/). It is unclear why the copula includes /m/ and not /n/ as is found in line 8 and in the other PWG lects. The nature of the /m/ is weakly articulated as well, pronounced like Leslau's spirantized nasals elsewhere in Gurage. Also, the glottal and vowel before the nasal are unexpected.

The auxiliary existential is shortened in 12 to /bɑ/, as noted in the discussion for line 6.

The verb 'to bless' is in the imperfect form here, 'when + 3M + bless + 3MPL', with both agreement affixes (the prefix and the suffix) agreeing with the subject (polite—plural). The /-uwɛ-/ suffix is expected; Leslau notes the same in Endegeny (1992:468). The k/t/d final suffix, in this environment /-t/, is known to appear on temporal verbs: "the most general and fundamental temporal form is t + imperfect + [k/t/d sfx] in PWG" (Hetzron 1977:101).

As in line 11, the 3M prefix in the imperfect, when following the temporal /t-/, is raised to /i/. There is only the most minimal stress on the final syllable of the verb /wɛ : r-ˈɛ/ 'went', yet it does appear

Appendix D

to be functioning as a converb. The verb appears to be another example of the durative-habitual past here as found above in 10.

The Mesmes word 'to go/to pass' /wɛ : rɛ/ is identical to the other PWG languages. The lengthened vowel is not found outside of PWG: Cheha /wɛrɛ-m/, Ezha /wɛrɛ-m/, Ennemor /wɛ : rɛ/, Endegeny /wɛ : rɛ/, and Gyeto /wɛ : rɛ/ (Leslau 1979).

Line 13:

See the notes on line 6 for comments regarding the possibility of the verb stem /k'ɛbbɛr/'to plant' entering Mesmes through borrowing from another Gurage language. The stress marked on the final syllables of the verbs /aggɛl-'ɛ/ 'raised cattle' and /k'ɛbbɛr-'ɛ/ 'planted' is indicative of what Hetzron calls the /-m/ converb (1977:94). For a discussion of this construction, see the note for line 6. Etically, the stress sounds like gemination of the final consonant radical.

The Mesmes word for 'poor' (nominal), /ɨze : gɛ/, is clearly a reflex of the Gurage etymon: Cheha /zega/, Ezha /zega/, Ennemor /zi : ga/, Endegeny /zi : gɛ/, Gyeto /ze : ga/ (Leslau 1979), though the first vowel does not show the heightening innovation seen in Ennemor and Endegeny. The verb 'be sated' in Central West Gurage (CWG) is /t'ɛfʷɛ-m/ and /t'ɛffʷɛ-m/ and in Ennemor and Endegeny: /ʔofʷɛ/ and /ʔoffɛ/, respectively. It is likely that the backing of the vowel in PWG (including Mesmes) is due to left-spreading labialization which then must surface on the vowel since the glottalized stop debuccalizes.

Line 14:

The /t-/ temporal on the verb /t-i-mowɛd/ 'when he died' is actually pronounced like the voiced affricate [d͡ʒ], probably due to the fast speech and heavily voiced, heavily palatalized environment. The verb 'to die' in CWG is /mʷɛtɛ-m/ but in PWG, the vowel is rounded (backed) due to the /w/ which is then lost (this is akin to the process hypothesized above, in the note on line 13). The stem vowel is geminate in PWG: /mo : dɛ/ (Ennemor and Endegeny) and /mo : tɛ/ (Gyeto) (Leslau 1979). Mesmes has retained the /w/ and thus the vowel is not lengthened; it is my opinion that intervocalic

/w/'s are often lost in these languages and that this innovation is not necessarily indicative of shared history. As expected, the /t/ → /d/ voicing is evident in Ennemor, Endegeny, and Mesmes.

The Mesmes word meaning 'like' /hukko/ appears related to the reflex found in Muher, Mesqan, and Zway, respectively: /ɨkki/, /ɨkkɑ/, and /ukku/, meaning 'like this' according to Leslau's dictionary (1979). The other word in this construction, /hɑ : mmɛdɛ/, may be related to the Endegeny /wɑm : ɨhɛ/, meaning 'like this' (Leslau 1979). It must be admitted, however, that the sorts of alternations between the Endegeny and Mesmes words here are not attested elsewhere in the data. Thus, it is impossible to say for certain what the origin of this lexeme is. It is also possible that the word /hɑ : m : ɛdɛ/ could be parsed as 'that-be-SFX'. In this case, the nasal would be interpreted as the bound copula and the suffix would be from the k/t/d reflex.

The Mesmes word for 'to pay tax' /gebbɛr/ shows the same initial vowel change from /ɛ/ to /e/ attested in Endegeny; elsewhere in Gurage (including Ennemor) the /g/ is a prepalatal and the vowel is /ɛ/. The prepalatal series is lost in Endegeny and Mesmes. The gemination is the same as in Endegeny. This word is marked as a converb in the text.

I have been unable to determine the meaning of the Mesmes word /tuiʔioi/ and the morpheme breaks as they appear in the text are mere hypotheses based on parsing elsewhere in the text: /t-uiʔio-i/.

Line 15:

At the outset of line 15, the clause-chain continues with two additional converbs before the final clause 'I lived like that'. On the verb 'to guard cattle', see the note on line 1.

In Ennemor, the copula (minus the agreement prefix) is /-hẽ : r̃/ (Hetzron 1977:238, line 9 in text 20). Thus, the expected form for the copula in Mesmes would be (also minus the agreement prefix) essentially the same. But given that Mesmes, except for very few exceptions, disprefers nasalized vowels, nasalization in other PWG languages is often manifest as an actual nasal consonant, as seen

Appendix D 131

here in the Mesmes copula: /-hɛnɛr/. There is also the strong possibility that the nasal is archaic here and that the loss of the /n/ resulted in the vocalic length and nasalization found in Ennemor. As in Hetzron's texts, the copula may be used for 'live' as well as 'be'. The form /nɛppɛrɛ/ may be used for 'live'. This is the imperfect (non-past) form.

Line 16:

Hetzron writes, regarding demonstratives: "PWG has waa/haa preceding a noun, but waada/haada without a noun" (1977:57). This initial /bɑ-hɑ : dɑ wɑ : dɑ/ appears to show both forms of the demonstrative pronoun in PWG. My translation 'after all that' in appendix C is what is preferred by my Ennemor contacts.

The word /mɛngist/ 'government' is a loan from Amharic, መንግሥት /mɛngist/.

Again, as in line 4, the relative clause marker is /ɛ-/, as expected in PWG (1977:98). But in this example the relative clause is lacking the k/t/d suffix, unlike the example in line 4. The 1PL /n/ agreement marker undergoes assimilation and is pronounced as a velar nasal before a /g/.

On the verb 'pay taxes', see note on line 14.

The Mesmes word for 'be bound' is /ti-n-t-akkɨd/. Here, the passive marker /t-/ is prefixed to the root. The Mesmes example shows the devoicing of the /g → k/ as well as the gemination maintenance in accordance with Endegeny: Cheha /agɛdɛ-m/, Ezha /aggɛdɛ-m/, Ennemor /akɛdɛ/, Endegeny /akkɛdɛ/, Gyeto /akɛdɛ/ (Leslau 1979).

I was unable to find a source for the Mesmes verb root /t'ɛd/ 'be released' or 'be free' in /t ɨ-n-t'ɛd/. Gurage does have /ftr/ 'be loosed' but this seems an unlikely source, since both the f and r would have to be lost in Mesmes and this is by no means a typical change between the varieties.

It is likely that in the second half of line 16 /tɨ-n-t-ɑkkɨd tɨ-n-t'ɛd/ is idiomatic; I have not been able to determine the specific meaning here.

Line 17:

The Mesmes word for 'likewise' /mɨhɛmɨʔ/ is possibly related to the forms /ɨm : ɛxɛ/ in Ennemor or /wɑm : ɨhɛ/ meaning 'like' in Endegeny (Leslau 1979).

Both the verbs /tʃʷɔd-ɛh-ˈi : / 'to plow' and /wɑʔɑr-ɛhʷ-ˈi : / 'to guard cattle' are inflected for the purposive (Hetzron 1977:99) as well as the converb (the latter marked with the stressing of the final /-i/ vowel). See notes on line 6 for more on the purposive.

The deverbal formation /geb : ɨri-nn-itɛ/ 'farming' is interesting. Leslau, in his dictionary (1979), does not list the verb root /gbr/ as associated with ploughing or farming in Gurage, only paying taxes. It may be that the word here has been borrowed from Amharic. The copula /-n-/ is clearly geminate here, but that is unexpected. Hetzron does not mention the bound copula nasal geminating in PWG languages. It does, however, appear to be geminate in Muher, at times (1977:109). The copula in Mesmes is the penultimate element, as expected (1977:106), followed by the expected -t suffix (see note on line 8).

Line 18:

The Mesmes verb for 'to spend the night' is unique to Ennemor-Endegeny-Mesmes subgroup. The Mesmes word is identical to the Endegeny, having palatalized the initial /n/: Cheha /ɑdɛrɛ-m/ or /ɑtɛrɛ/, Ezha /ɑdɛrɛ-m/, Ennemor /neʔɛ/, Endegeny /ɲɛʔɛ/, Gyeto /ɑtɛrɛ/ (Leslau 1979). The verb is marked as a converb in the text.

The Mesmes existential verb in line 18 is the same as the word in Ennemor and Endegeny. In Mesmes, the gemination is maintained as it is in Endegeny: Cheha /nɛrɛ/, Ezha /nɛrɛ/, Ennemor /ɑnɛ/, Endegeny /ɑnnɛ/, Gyeto /nɛrɛ/ (Leslau 1979). This existential-locative, as Hetzron calls it (1977:108), "is conjugated as a perfect, [but]

Appendix D 133

has a present tense meaning and may have the prefix /t-/ 'when' which otherwise appears before the imperfect only."

Line 19:

The beginning of line 19 contains an apparent idiom for 'back in the old days'. The word /duro/ is 'formerly' in Leslau's (1979) dictionary; the /u/ vowel is found only in Endegeny and Zway. The first vowel is /ɨ/ elsewhere in Western Gurage. The initial vowel, set off with parentheses, is most likely epenthetic, required between the two coronals. The expected shape for the genitive prefix would be /a-/, according to my reading of Hetzron's Ennemor texts (1977). In the Mesmes word /gaʔat/ 'dawn' (a nominal), Mesmes certainly shows the same change as Endegeny: Cheha /gɑt/, Ezha /gɑtt/, Ennemor /gɑʔat/, Endegeny /gɑʔat/, Gyeto /gɑʔat/ (Leslau 1979). The Mesmes word /zɛm/ is found in Leslau's (1979) dictionary, meaning 'period of time'. Cognates are found throughout Gurage: Cheha /zɛbɛr/, Ezha /zɛbɛr/, Ennemor /zẽm̥ɛr/, Endegeny /zɛ : n/, Gyeto /zɛm̥ɛr̃/[2] (1979).

The /b-/ prefix is used on verbs to mark conditionals as well as temporals (1977:104–106); it is also used on nouns to mark location (in), accompaniment (with) and instrumental (by means of). In line 19, the /b-/ prefix is on the quantifier /ɑwnst/, marking instrumental. See Hetzron's Ennemor text #20 (1977:237) for a clear example containing many of these uses.

The numeral 'five' in Mesmes has an initial /h-/ in Bender's (1969) wordlist, which was dropped when the /b-/ prefix was added in the text. See footnote 57 in 4.2.4. on the loss of initial laryngeals in Gurage and their maintenance in Mesmes. The final vowel /-e/ is dropped, as expected, in connected speech. These two changes aside, there are still differences between the shape of the Mesmes numeral in the text and its shape in Bender's wordlist: text /hawnste/ wordlist /ha : nste/. Leslau's dictionary provides the Endegeny numeral 'five' which helps to explain the history: /ã : wɨst/ and /ã : st/. Both these forms are recorded as Endegeny. Here, it is clear that the /m/ has weakened to the /w/, or in the other example, lost altogether, and the nasalization has been maintained on

---

[2] As mentioned above, the diacritic under the /m/ is meant to show weak articulation (see section 4.2.4.1).

the vowel. In Mesmes, by contrast, the nasal is maintained as a full consonant, not a suprasegmental feature—this is a common difference between Mesmes and Ennemor/Endegeny (see note on line 15).

The Mesmes word for 'women' (in the plural) is /e : ʃi/. As expected, Mesmes shares with Endegeny the change from final /-a/, but without the nasalization found in Endegeny. The final vowel in Mesmes is raised due to the palatal, a common process encountered throughout this text: Cheha /iʃta/, Ezha /iʃta/, Ennemor /ɨʃtʃa/, Endegeny /ẽ : ʃɛ/, Gyeto /iʃta/or /iʃtʃa/ (Leslau 1979).

The final verb 'to give birth' is marked as main past by the final stressed vowel (see note on line 4).

Line 20:

I have been unable to determine the meaning of the Mesmes word /wɛdkɛ/. No cognate has been found elsewhere in Gurage for words that fit the particular context, such as 'all' or 'total'.

As seen elsewhere, the main verbs are only inconsistently marked with the k/t/d suffix. In this case, /ʔeɲɲ-uwɛ-tu/ 'to give birth' carries the suffix.

The numeral 'twenty' in Mesmes (discussed in greater detail in 4.2.4.4) shows the same vowel change due to the labialization, which then drops in both Endegeny and Mesmes. It also shows the same metathesis phenomenon: Cheha /xʷɨja/, Ezha /xʷɨjja/, Ennemor /xʷijʔa/, Endegeny /huʔjɛ/, Gyeto /xʷɨja/ (Leslau 1979).

Due to the form of the verb 'to live', it is my opinion that this is a borrowing from Amharic ኖረ /nor-ɛ/ 'lived-3MS'. The expected PWG reflex is /nɛp : ɛrɛ/, which is cognate with the Amharic past existential ነበረ /nɛbbɛr-ɛ/ 'EXIST-3MS'.

Appendix E

Gurage language survey Map with Principal Towns

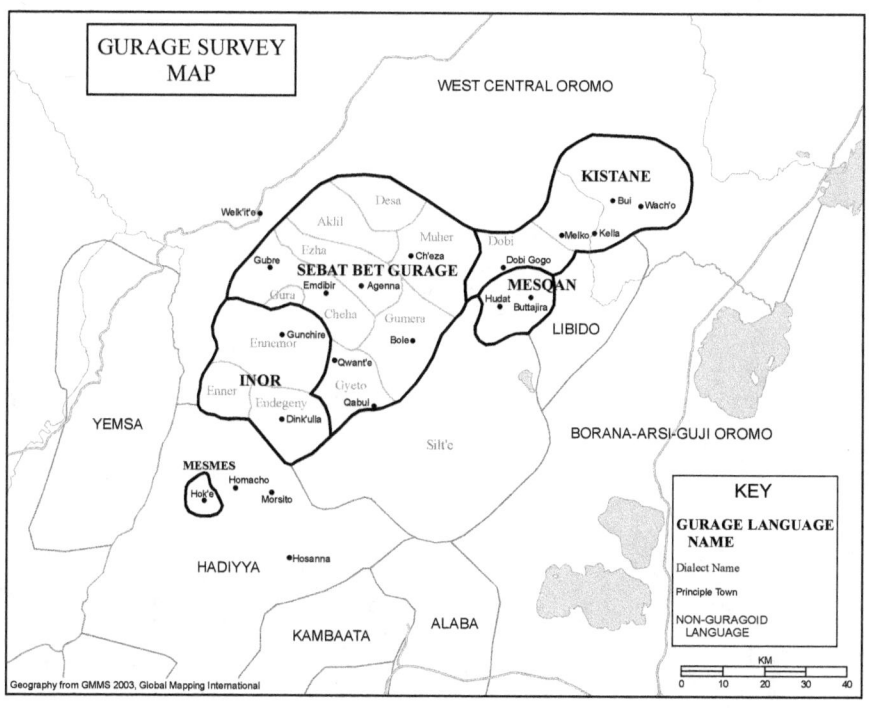

References

Ahland, Colleen. 2003. Interlectal intelligibility between Gurage speech varieties. Paper presented at the 31st annual meeting of North American Conference on Afroasiatic Linguistics, Nashville.

Ahland, Michael. 2006. Nasal spreading, rhinoglottophilia and the genesis of a non-etymological nasal consonant in Mesmes. In Rebecca T. Cover and Yuni Kim (eds.), *Proceedings of the thirty-first annual meeting of the Berkeley Linguistics Society*, 13–24. Berkeley: Berkeley Linguistics Society.

Ahland, Michael and Colleen Ahland. 2001. Gurage language survey report. ms.

Bailey, C.-J. 1996. *Essays on Time-Based Linguistic Analysis*. Oxford: Clarendon Press.

Bender, M. L. 1969. Unpublished fieldnotes on Mesmes.

Bender, M. L. 1971. The languages of Ethiopia: A new lexicostatistic classification and some problems of diffusion. *Journal of Anthropological Linguistics* 13:165–288.

Bender, M. L. 1997. Upside-down Afrasian. *Afrikanistische Arbeitspapiere* 50:19–34.

Blust, Robert. 1998. Seimat vowel nasality: A typological anomaly. *Oceanic Linguistics* 37(2):298–322.

Boivin, Robert. 1996. Spontaneous nasalization in Inor. In Grover Hudson (ed.), *Essays on Gurage language and culture, dedicated to Wolf Leslau on the occasion of his 90th birthday*, 21–33. Wiesbaden: Harrassowitz.

Brenzinger, Matthias, Bernd Heine, and Gabriele Sommer. 1991. Language death in Africa. In R. H. Robins and E. M. Uhlenbeck (eds.), *Endangered languages*, 19–44. Providence, R.I.: Berg Publishers.

Brenzinger, Matthias and Gerrit Dimmendaal, eds. 1992. *Language death: Factual and theoretical explorations with special reference to East Africa.* Berlin and New York: Mouton de Gruyter.

Campbell, Lyle. 2004. *Historical linguistics: An introduction,* Second edition. Cambridge, Mass.: MIT Press.

Campbell, Lyle and Martha C. Muntzel. 1989. The structural consequences of language death. In Nancy Dorian (ed.), *Investigating obsolescence,* 181–196. Cambridge: Cambridge University Press.

Casad, Eugene H. 1974. *Dialect intelligibility testing.* Norman: Summer Institute of Linguistics and the University of Oklahoma.

Central Statistical Authority. 1994. *Population and housing census of Ethiopia.* Addis Ababa: Central Statistical Authority.

Cerulli, Enrico. 1936. *Studi Etiopici. I. La lingua e la storia di Harar.* Rome.

Cohen, Marcel. 1931. *Études d'Éthiopien méridional.* Paris: Librairie Orientaliste Paul Geuthner / Libraire de la Société Asiatique.

Comrie, Bernard. 1976. *Aspect.* Cambridge Textbooks in Linguistics. Cambridge: Cambridge University Press.

Cooper, Robert L. and Susan Carpenter. 1976. In M. L. Bender, J. D. Bowen, R. L. Cooper, and C. A. Ferguson (eds.), *Language in the market. Language in Ethiopia,* 244–255. New York: Oxford University Press.

Dorian, Nancy. 1977. The problem of the semi-speaker in language death. Language death. In Joshua Fishman (ed.), *International Journal of the Sociology of Language,* 12:23–32. The Hague-Paris-New York: Mouton.

Dressler, Wolfgang. 1991. The sociolinguistic and patholinguistic attrition of Breton phonology, morphology and morphonology. In Herbert W. Seliger and Robert M. Vago (eds), *First language attrition,* 99–112. Cambridge: Cambridge University Press.

Dressler, Wolfgang and Ruth Wodak-Leodolter. 1977a. Introduction. Language death. *International Journal of the Sociology of Language* 12:5–11.

Dressler, Wolfgang and Ruth Wodak-Leodolter. 1977b. Language preservation and language death in Brittany. Language death. *International Journal of the Sociology of Language* 12:33–44.

Faber, Alice. 1997. Genetic subgrouping of the Semitic languages. In Robert Hetzron (ed.), *The Semitic languages,* 3–13. New York: Routledge.

References

Faingold, Eduardo. 1996. *Child language, creolization, and historical change: Spanish in contact with Portuguese.* Tübingen: G. Narr.

Ferguson, Charles A. 1976. The Ethiopian language area. In M. L. Bender, J. D. Bowen, R. L. Cooper and C. A. Ferguson (eds.), Language in Ethiopia. 63–76. London: Oxford University Press.

Fishman, Joshua A. 1989. *Language and ethnicity in minority sociolinguistic perspective.* Clevedon and Philadelphia: Multilingual Matters.

Girma A. Demeke. 2001. The Ethio-Semitic languages (re-examining the classification). *Journal of Ethiopian Studies* 24:57–93.

Grimes, Joseph. 1995. *Language survey reference guide.* Dallas: Summer Institute of Linguistics.

Gutt, Ernst-August. 1977. Intelligibility and interlingual comprehension among selected Gurage speech varieties. *Journal of Ethiopian Studies* 14:216–232.

Hetzron, Robert. 1972. *Ethiopian Semitic studies in classification.* Manchester: University Press.

Hetzron, Robert. 1976. Two principles of genetic reconstruction. *Lingua* 38:89–108.

Hetzron, Robert. 1977. *The Gunnän-Gurage languages.* Instituto Orientale Di Napoli.

Hudson, Grover. 1976. Highland East Cushitic. In M. L. Bender (ed.), *The Non-Semitic languages of Ethiopia*, 232–277. East Lansing: African Studies Center, Michigan State University.

Hudson, Grover. 1977. Language classification and the Semitic prehistory of Ethiopia. *Folia Orientalia* 18:119–166.

Hudson, Grover. 2000. Ethiopian Semitic overview. *Journal of Ethiopian Studies* 13:75–86.

Hudson, Grover. 2002. Ethiopian Semitic archaic heterogeneity. *Proceedings, 14th International Conference of Ethiopian Studies* 3:1765–1776.

International Phonetic Association. 1999. *Handbook of the International Phonetic Association: A guide to the use of the International Phonetic Alphabet.* Cambridge: Cambridge University Press.

Leslau, Wolf. 1945. The influence of Cushitic on the Semitic languages of Ethiopia: A problem of substratum. *Word* 1:59–82.

Leslau, Wolf. 1959. Sidamo features in the South Ethiopic phonology. *Journal of the American Oriental Society* 79:1–7.

Leslau, Wolf. 1965. Is there a Proto-Gurage? *Proceedings of the International Conference on Semitic Studies,* 152–171. Jerusalem: Israel Academy of Sciences and Humanities.

Leslau, Wolf. 1968. *The land of Prester John*. Los Angeles: University of California Press.

Leslau, Wolf. 1969. Toward a classification of the Gurage dialects. *Journal of Semitic Studies* 14:96–109.

Leslau, Wolf. 1970. Classification of the Semitic Languages of Ethiopia. *Proceedings from the 3rd International Conference of Ethiopian Studies* 2:5–25.

Leslau, Wolf. 1979. *Etymological dictionary of Gurage (Ethiopic)*. Wiesbaden: Otto Harrassowitz.

Leslau, Wolf. 1992a. *Gurage studies: Collected articles*. Wiesbaden: Otto Harrassowitz.

Leslau, Wolf. 1992b. The verb forms in Endegeny. In Leslau 1992a, 160–169.

Leslau, Wolf. 1992c. Nasalization in the East Gurage group of Semitic Ethiopic. In Leslau 1992a, 263.

Leslau, Wolf. 1992d. Traces of the laryngeals in Endegen. In Leslau 1992a, 288–297.

Leslau, Wolf. 1992e. The influence of Sidamo on the Ethiopic languages of Gurage. In Leslau 1992a, 260–278.

Leslau, Wolf. 1996. Čaha and Ennemor: An analysis of two Gurage dialects. In Grover Hudson (ed.), *Essays on Gurage language and culture, dedicated to Wolf Leslau on the occasion of his 90th birthday*, 111–122. Weisbaden: Harrassowitz.

Maher, Julianne. 1991. A crosslinguistic study of language contact and language attrition. In Herbert W. Seliger and Robert M.Vago (eds.), *First language attrition*, 67–84. Cambridge: Cambridge University Press.

Matisoff, James. 1975. Rhinoglottophilia: The mysterious connection between nasalityand glottality. In Charles Ferguson, Larry M. Hyman, and John Ohala (eds.), *Nasalfest: Papers from a symposium on nasals and nasalization*, 265–287 Stanford, California: Stanford University Language Universals Project.

Menn, Lise. 1989. Some people who don't talk right: Universal and particular in child language, aphasia, and language obsolescence. In Nancy C. Dorian (ed.), *Investigating obsolescence: Studies in language contraction and death*, 335–345. Cambridge: Cambridge University Press.

Michailovsky, Boyd. 1975. A case of rhinoglottophilia in Hayu. *Linguistics of the Tibeto-Burman Area* 2(2):293.

Murtonen, A. 1967. Early Semitic, a diachronical inquiry into the relationship of Ethiopic to the other so-called south-east Semitic languages. In G. F. Pijper (ed), *Studies in Semitic languages and linguistics 1*. Leiden: E. J. Brill.

Naigzy Gebremedhin. 1971. Some traditional types of housing in Ethiopia. In Paul Oliver (ed.), *Shelter in Africa*, 106–123. New York: Praeger.

Parker, Stephen George. 1996. Toward a universal form for 'yes': or, rhinoglottophiliaand the affirmation grunt. *Journal of Linguistic Anthropology* 6:85–95.

Rose, Sharon. 2003. Durational constraints on Engegeň gemination. Paper presented at the 15th International Conference of Ethiopian Studies, July 20–25, 2003, Hamburg University, Germany.

Sasse, Hans-Jurgen. 1992a. Theory of language death. In Matthias Brenzinger (ed.), *Language death: Factual and theoretical explorations with special reference to East Africa*, 7–30. Berlin and New York: Morton de Gruyter.

Sasse, Hans-Jurgen. 1992b. Language decay and contact-induced change. In Matthias Brenzinger (ed.), *Language death: Factual and theoretical explorations with special reference to East Africa*, 59–80. Berlin and New York: Morton de Gruyter.

Seliger, Herbert W. and Robert M. Vago. 1991. The study of first language attrition: An overview. In Herbert W. Seliger and Robert M.Vago, eds., 3–15.

Seliger, Herbert W. and Robert M. Vago, eds. 1991. *First language attrition*. Cambridge: Cambridge University Press.

Shack, William A. 1966. *The Gurage: A people of the ensete culture*. London: Oxford University Press.

Sim, Ronnie. 1988. Violations of the two-consonant constraint in Hadiyya. *African Languages and Culture* 1:77–90.

Sim, Ronnie. 1989. Predicate conjoining in Hadiyya. University of Edinburgh. Unpublished dissertation.

Stinson, D. Lloyd. 1976. Hadiyya. In M. L. Bender, J. D. Bowen, R. L. Cooper, and C. A. Ferguson (eds.), *Language in Ethiopia*, 148–154. London: Oxford University Press.

Thomason, Sarah and Terrence Kaufman. 1988. *Language contact, creolization, and genetic linguistics*. Berkeley and Los Angeles: University of California Press.

Thomason, Sarah G. 2001. *Language contact: An introduction*. Washington, D.C.: Georgetown University Press.

Ullendorff, Edward. 1960. *The Ethiopians*. Oxford: Oxford University Press.
UPenn. 1995. http://www.africa.upenn.edu/eue_web/soup_may.htm. Accessed 12 February 2008.
Wurm, Stephen A. 1991. Language death and disappearance: Causes and circumstances. In R. H. Robins and E. M. Uhlenbeck (eds.), *Endangered languages*, 1–18. Providence, R.I.: Berg Publishers Limited.
Zaborski, Andrzej. 1991. Ethiopian language subareas. Unwritten testimonies of the African past. In Stanislaw, Pilaszewicz, and Eugeniusz Rzewuski (eds.), *Proceedings of the International Symposium held in Ojrzanów, Warsaw on November 7–8, 1989*, 123–134. Warsaw: Wydawnictwa Uniwersytetu Warszawskiego.

SIL International and
The University of Texas at Arlington
Publications in Linguistics

Recent Publications

144. **The phonology of two central Chadic languages**, by Tony Smith and Richard Gravina. 2009.
143. **A grammar of Akoose: A northwest Bantu language**, by Robert Hedinger. 2008.
142. **Word order in Toposa: An aspect of multiple feature-checking**, by Helga Schröder. 2008.
141. **Aspects of the morphology and phonology of Konni**, by Michael C. Cahill. 2007.
140. **The phonology of Mono**, by Kenneth S. Olson. 2005.
139. **Language and life: Essays in memory of Kenneth L. Pike**, ed. by Mary Ruth Wise, Thomas N. Headland, and Ruth M. Brend. 2003.
138. **Case and agreement in Abaza**, by Brian O'Herin. 2002.
137. **Pragmatics of persuasive discourse of Spanish television advertising**, by Karol J. Hardin. 2001.
136. **Quiegolani Zapotec syntax: A Principles and parameters account**, by Cheryl A. Black. 2000.
135. **A grammar of Sochiapan Chinantec: Studies in Chinantec languages 6**, by David Paul Foris. 2001.

International Academic Bookstore
SIL International
7500 W. Camp Wisdom Road
Dallas, TX 75236-5699

Voice: 972-708-7404
Fax: 972-708-7363
Email: academic_books@sil.org
Internet: http://www.ethnologue.com
International Academic Bookstore
SIL International
7500 W. Camp Wisdom Road
Dallas, TX 75236-5699

www.ingramcontent.com/pod-product-compliance
Lightning Source LLC
Chambersburg PA
CBHW070338240426
43665CB00045B/2226